IDENTITY

CRISIS

'Unlock The Hidden Treasure Within You'

Shingie Fundira

DEAN THOMPSON
Publishing

Dear Shy,

Thanks for the love and support.

love
Shingie.

Contents

Pre Identity Crisis Questions

"What defines a person as a unique individual? A natural disposition? A face? A vocabulary of gestures? Are we born individuals or do we mould ourselves into unique creatures through our experiences and accomplishments? Every human enters the world with a vast, incalculable potential. But myriad factors invariably conspire to prevent us from fully achieving that potential." **– Ezra C Daniels**

Here are some questions to help you with your identity crisis endeavour:

1. Who am I?
2. What is my identity?
3. What do I want out of life?
4. Where do I see myself physically, mentally, and spiritually in the next few hours, days, weeks, months and years to come?
5. What is my current status: health, finance, career, relationships, friends and family?
6. What do I believe in?
7. What do I want and what do I need?
8. What are my expectations?
9. What makes me happy and what makes me sad?
10. What are my weaknesses and what are my strengths?
11. How far am I willing to go to change my life?
12. Who am I?

Warning: You are going to be faced with a lot of personal and maybe offensive questions in this book. I will let you peel your own onion layers as you see fit. After you finish reading the book, I encourage you to come back and attempt these questions again.

Good luck!

Publisher's Note

Shingie Fundira's debut non-fiction, inspirational book is a novelty. It is well written and the book moves at a cracking pace - it never lets up for a moment.

In this world of outrage that we are living, this is a timely, poignant and deep book that should be on everyone's shelf.

It is centred on an inherent contradiction within our need for self-worth, self-recognition and the desire to fit-in into a society that is inherently complex – a society characterised by what she calls 'cultural resistance, ignorance or traditional manipulation'.

We crave to be seen as both equal and superior to others and this causes us to live in the 'shadow of our real identity'.

In just twelve chapters Shingie captures what many have called Hegel's dialectic where the two forces of individualism and the desire to be part of society or community, are irreconcilable, yet are also inseparable.

We are individuals whose entire life is defined by the identity of our communities and therefore fail to explore or 'unlock' what Shingie calls 'the hidden treasure within you'.

Without being overly prescriptive, Shingie offers a brief set of 12 questions which will make you think about how to overcome the danger of identity crisis.

She urges us to 'identify our identity crisis' and says 'who you really are is the primary step to unlocking the hidden treasure within you'.

These recommendations help us to navigate this 'bewildering thing called life'. After all, our 'mortal body is only living on borrowed time. Tomorrow is not guaranteed'.

Itayi Garande

No 1 bestselling author of 'Reconditioning: Change your life in one minute'

Author's Note

"Character is like pregnancy. It cannot be hidden forever"
–African proverb

Identity crisis is a real "crisis" that undeniably affects you and I in one way or another. This crisis was, this crisis is, and this crisis will be around for as long as you and I exist. There are several approaches to an identity crisis. You may choose to accept it, embrace it and work on it. You may remain naïve or oblivious to its existence, or you may just simply deny having any form of an identity crisis. You may have been designed to think that life is what it is; henceforth you will never fully concede that you have any identity crisis. Moreover, you may unfortunately fall under an oppressive and manipulative cultural bracket that deters you from freely portraying your true identity. If you come from a hard-core traditional or religious family, the aforementioned bracket is often attached to one of the famous biblical Ten Commandments, "Honour your father and your mother."

When it comes to identity crisis, I personally think that "Honour your father and your mother" is one of the most misused and abused scriptures by what I perceive to be misinformed individuals. The actual text versus the context of this commandment is often used to crush one's real identity (morals and beliefs) by instilling fear, or imposing manipulative threats such as, "You will never make it in life unless you honour everything I say." This is quite common within the Afro-Caribbean cultures.

They say the mouth of an elderly man is without teeth, but never without words of wisdom. The bible says, "Lack of knowledge will make my people perish" (Hosea 4:6 KJV). Therefore, if you do not know what you are supposed to know in order to survive, then you will surely perish mentally, spiritually, emotionally and psychologically.

Nonetheless, I beg to differ about every elderly person. Just because they are elderly, it does not necessarily mean that they all possess the appropriate wisdom, knowledge and understanding about life. They could be an elderly fool, full of nonsense. Some of them made their own decisions to live the way they do. They probably did not agree with most of the imposed decisions on them, however, the fact is they still chose to go wherever the wind blew. Now they want to impose their identity crisis on to the next generation - YOU. Their lack of self-awareness and identity made them who they are today. Their fear and lack of knowledge plays a significant part of their identity crisis.

So what?

You have to reconnect and recondition your way of thinking. You have to engage in some thought-provoking habits in order to dismantle any culpable rituals that have been keeping you in any form of an identity crisis bondage. If you negate the fact that there's a lot of potential within you, that there's a lot of hidden treasure within you waiting to be discovered, extracted and put to good use, you may never get to experience the real you. You will continue to be a shadow of your real identity.

I can assertively attest to enduring a lot of trials, tribulations, misfortunes, setbacks, and disappointments. However, I came to the realisation that no matter the identity crisis, I can do all things through Christ which strengthens me. That means if I had allowed myself to remain bound in any form of identity crisis, my mind would constantly be populated with limiting beliefs. Inherently, the limited mind-set would conversely control my future and destiny.

I would become nothing and feel nothing. So I allowed God to open and activate all my stagnant spiritual senses; to let me be the head and not the tail, to order all my steps and to make a way where there seems to be no way. I continue to encourage myself in the Lord as I progressively unlock the hidden treasure within me.

As a unique individual, you have to clear some things that may deter your progression in doing what you are called to do. Cleanse your mind, body and soul daily; stretch yourself and lengthen your cords. Life is a journey; fasten your seatbelt as you live, laugh, and love, and do not forget to enjoy the ride.

Dedication

My late great grandmother used to say to me, "If everything in your life seems flawless, effortless and too good to be true, expect the road ahead to be problematic at some point. However, if you experience some challenges, some trials and tribulations along the way, then your life is in the right direction."

I never fully understood this remark until I was old enough to appreciate her profound wisdom and knowledge. She was a special kind of "they – the elderly."

I honestly thought she meant that I was compelled to suffer and struggle in order to attain good fortune in life. In due course, I found out that the challenges she talked about were hidden in the various forms of identity crisis. Her piercing words of wisdom have since moulded my paths and directed the way I navigate my life. I am in constant touch with my natural and spiritual make up – my real identity. Thank you grandmother and may your soul continue to rest in eternal peace.

Mum – You have single-handedly been the pillar of strength all my life. There's never a time you let me go without anything I needed. They say the apple does not fall too far from the tree – I guess they were right. I love you and thank you mum.

Marigold – our occasional sister-sister catch-ups always keep me energised as you always have something up your sleeve. You encouraged me to keep going and to keep chasing my dreams. Thank you baby sister.

To the P-Power team, you guys have no idea how you always kick start my mornings. You are definitely second to my coffee addiction. Lol. Thank you guys for all the love and support.

To everyone I nagged whilst working on this book, you will always have that special place in my heart. Thank you for lending an ear and being a shoulder to cry on when it was immensely required. Let's keep winning together.

Introduction

"It was the best of times, it was the worst of times, it was the age of wisdom, it was the age of foolishness, it was the epoch of belief, and it was the epoch of incredulity" – **Charles Dickens**

Have you ever been lost whilst behind the wheel, found yourself at a crossroad or spaghetti junction and deliberated which direction to take? At this point, a road map, satnav or compass to point out the cardinal direction would be an ideal solution to this dilemma wouldn't it?

Have you ever tried to solve a Rubik Cube's multi-coloured sequence with minimal effort and less muddling, so that all the squares on each side are of the same colour? At first glance, it looks quite modest and easy until a few failed twisting and turning attempts. Your initial contemplation on which colour combination to elucidate first suddenly becomes an identity crisis.

Have you ever tried to comprehend this bewildering thing called "life" several times? You question your existence, your purpose and your final destiny on this earth. You question evolution versus creation. You question survival versus adaptation. You question the inevitable death versus the afterlife. Ideally, you seem to question everything. In as much as you try to figure out the in-between, you soon realise that your mortal body is only living on borrowed time. Tomorrow is not guaranteed. You start to go through several changes, some of which include burying family and friends due to "life happens." The Covid-19 pandemic has certainly proved to be part of the classic "life happens" proclamation.

The "life happens" baffles the human mind because you will never know when your turn will come. Ecclesiastes 3:2 states, 'There's a time to be born and a time to die.' If only it could give us an estimated time of death, so that we could try and do this life thing intentionally, and be fully prepared to figure it all out. Prince EA, a powerful YouTube motivational speaker once said, "Every one dies, but not everyone lives." This profound statement implies that a lot of us are short-changing ourselves until it is rather too late to start living life. So, do you want to figure out life on your deathbed or do you want to identify yourself now and fully embrace the gift of life?

Have you ever had your dreams completely shut down because of cultural resistance, ignorance or traditional manipulation? You are constantly told that you will not make it in life no matter how hard you try. You have to go for a "chosen" career path because 'they – the elders' know what's good for you, and your future. Besides, 'they – the elders' are paying for it, and because you live under their roof, you either take it or you leave it. Basically, 'they – the elders' forcefully choose your destiny for you. As you grow older, you find yourself wrestling with situations and circumstances you were compelled to augment incompetently.

Do you have so many unanswered questions in spite of how many wise, gifted and talented people you conversed with? Their extra-ordinary techniques and contributions persistently defied your culturally conditioned mind, and hence you continue to tussle with intuition. Moreover, you persistently struggle with the unavoidable identity crisis conundrum.

You and I have, to a certain extent, explored the inexhaustible and incisive "life" questions. Some of those questions were answered, whilst some remain an absolute mystery. Some help to identify limiting beliefs stressors and to form an action plan to move forward, whilst some simply cause more stress and anxiety.

I hope this read will help you to ascertain your identity crisis and provoke you enough to take action as you see fit. The time is now. Identify your identity crisis and unlock the hidden treasure within you.

Chapter 1

What Is An Identity Crisis?

"Are you broken? Good. Now fall apart completely. You will realize that what has fallen apart is not you. It's just a thin external coating that hides your pure, eternal and ever-shining being" **– Shunya**

I f you do not know who you are, you may naively allow anyone, anything and everything out there to delineate you. Character identification and building is primarily vital for appropriate life navigation and configuration. Lack of self-awareness can impede the knack to overcome some of the challenges you inevitably encounter on a day-to-day basis. You need to do regular self "M.O.Ts" (thorough self-checks) in order to self-reconcile, self-recondition and unlock the hidden "identity treasure" within you.

Trying to figure out one's real identity can, to a certain degree, be challenging, frustrating and perplexing. You will also encounter a lot of unforeseen circumstances. Identity crisis can be rendered in many ways which include mental-identity, physical-identity, natural-identity and spiritual-identity. Your ethnicity and socio-economic influences also play a fundamental part in solidifying your identity crisis.

This is either by default or through expository and learned behaviour.

German psychologist Erik Erikson coined identity crisis as the failure to achieve ego identity during adolescence. "The stage of psychosocial development in which identity crisis may occur is called the identity cohesion vs. role confusion. During this stage, adolescents are faced with physical growth, sexual maturity, and integrating ideas of themselves and about what others think of them."

The layman's definition of identity crisis is a period of uncertainty and confusion in which a person's sense of identity becomes apprehensive. This is typically due to transformation in their anticipated objectives or character in society. You may find that you struggle to fit in within diverse social groups because of character differences, interests and sentiments. You may possess extraversion or introversion traits or a certain degree of both. These traits influence how you relate with people or identify where you belong within a community.

Furthermore, your fashion-sense, cuisine-sense, career-sense, hobby-sense, financial-sense, relationship-sense and any extra activities-sense, may be demarcated by family role models or socialites that you follow on all the various social media platforms. You imitate how they dress, how they talk, how they live, and anything else that inspires you. Basically, all your senses and how you spend your time is governed by them.

Personality plays a huge part of your identity. Knowing who you really are is the primary step to unlocking the hidden treasure within you. Your character should develop and mature as you grow older. Conversely, for some it hardly develops and it, in fact, immatures and deteriorates. Character development takes time. As the saying goes, "Rome was not built in a day," and likewise, character building will take some ample time.

So what is your identity crisis? Does it involve things like love, friends, career, money, family, and other things you are still yet to discover on this life expedition? Well, as you begin to identify and to unlock your identity mysteries, it is imperative to know that your life is very different from another person. Therefore, you need to circumvent comparing and contrasting your identity crisis with anyone else, and this includes your own family. This is your journey, your life and your identity. The ball is in your court.

Chapter 2

The Love-dentity Crisis

What is love? Does true love exist? Why does love hurt so badly? Why is it so hard to find real love? Why is it hard to stay in love? Why can't I be loved for whom I am? How can I experience genuine love and recognize it without being remorseful? How do I detach and distance myself from toxic love efficaciously? How do I unlock the love token after going through a love-tsunami or love-whirlwind? Is there really a love-light at the end of the tunnel?

These are some of what I call the *love-dentity* crisis perspectives that cross the mind when I think about love. I am sure that you have been a victim of 'matters of the heart' in one way or the other. You and I have also fallen short of the love-glory by inevitably holding back, or making someone else pay for what other people did to us in the past. The love wounds we both encountered and carry could be a result of loss, depression, hurt, disappointment, sorrow, abuse, infidelity in the marriage, courtship, entanglement, or whatever relationship you were, or are currently in. You may have experienced tough or no love at all either as a child or an adult, and hence you struggle to comprehend what real love is.

The heart is a very delicate organ of the immune system. It is quite tender and fragile at the same time. Once it stops functioning, everything else connected to it is greatly affected, and it may eventually come to a halt. Therefore, the measure of damage control you experienced in the past, probably made you build a cold heart of stone. You also probably erected a "love-proof wall" higher and stronger than the infamous Trump's wall between the US and Mexico. This was all in an effort to make sure that no one ever breaks through it again. The million dollar question is, how deep was and is your love? And is this love-proof wall really beneficial and necessary to you?

You might be a hard-core lover who is constantly susceptible to the wrong relationships. You may have unavoidable attachments to toxic and to the wrong kind of lovers as well. You may not get on well with some family members or siblings due to some ongoing family politics. You may have conflicting working conditions with your work colleagues. You may have estranged relations with some of your friends for whatever reasons. You may not have a great relationship with your neighbours or those you fellowship with. The list of why things do not go well with love and in love for you is endless. Could all this be down to the lack of what is known as the agape love?

Agape love is the kind of love that commands you to love your neighbour as you love yourself; to love your enemies and to pray for those that persecute you. It requires you to forgive all those that have wronged you, and to also accept the apologies that you will never receive. Agape love is more than emotions, it looks beyond the negatives and the wrongs. It has no measure of faults or grudges. Agape love is the kind that speaks louder than words. It is demonstrated mostly in how you respond, how you react, and what action you take towards adversaries. Now, have you ever wondered why it can be quite challenging to show and share some agape love?

I have struggled a few times to keep it real with agape love. It took a while for me to grasp the entirety of its true meaning, and the impact it has towards those I mix and mingle with. I found out that there are a number of intangible factors that contribute to having a love-dentity crisis. These factors are all manifestations of the lack of the agape love, and they include rejection, rebellion, stubbornness, inferiority, selfishness, distrust, self-reliance, self-seeking, self-destruction, disobedience, fear, confusion and last, but not least, pride.

My personal top three love-dentity crisis limiting factors are confusion, fear and rejection.

The Confusion Factor

> When you are confused, you do not know what to do. You are basically on the fence, and full of mixed emotions. You cannot move on unless you break through this love confusion wall. You are a mixture of hot and cold. Hot mixed with cold produces lukewarm. Black mixed with white produces grey. Lukewarm or grey represents mixed feelings, thoughts, plans, ideologies, emotions, lifestyle and etc. You are neither here nor there. You are

fighting the good and the bad at the same time, and in the end you yield vague results. Confusion in love is a very dangerous zone to be in. It is a crazy warzone.

This zone is often populated with persistent mind battles that result in lowliness, depression, stress, anxiety, frustration, endless tears, and recurring break-ups and make-ups. This zone attains short-lived gratification followed by permanent regret. This confusion bracket allows you to be taken advantage of by others as you are naively vulnerable. Confusion will allow you to be blown in any direction due to lack of self-awareness and a sound mind. Confusion equals indecision. That is an absolute dead zone.

The Fear Factor

Fear is a very dangerous binding spirit that can easily attack you. Fear will emotionally, spiritually and naturally cripple your mind. It will deactivate the medulla oblongata – this is the base of the brain which directly controls breathing, blood flow, and other essential immune system functions. Fear will invade your heart, and partake in an unauthorised heart incision, and leave the caustic operative tools in there for the inevitable unbearable pain. Fear will have a board of directors (voices in your head), instigating limiting beliefs and fabricating negative connotations.

Fear to try and fail, and still keep trying, fear to trust again, fear of loyalty, fear of commitment, or fear to open up your heart again, may cost you the only opportunity of experiencing real love for the first time, or for the umpteenth time. Fear of getting your heart ripped apart again, fear of giving it another chance, fear of falling for the same frog or dog, fear of experiencing the butterflies again, and fear of........(insert your fear list here), could be part of your love-dentity crisis. Do you fear for your heart? Do you fear love? Why do you fear so much?

Well, here is some food for thought, "For God does not give us the spirit of fear, but of power, love and a sound mind." What does this mean to you and how can this help you deal with your fear?

The Rejection Factor

You are either a victim of rejection by others or you are a self-imposed victim. Yes, you may suffer from self-rejection, but you always find a way to blame others for it. The fact is that you do not even love yourself or know how to start loving yourself, yet you expect others to love you in a certain way. How is that possible? How does it even work? Nonetheless, you may be the hopeless lover that falls first and loves really hard, but is always misunderstood. You end up alone after all that love you invest in others.

The love you give out is never reciprocated. You even end up in repeated rejection cycles because you haven't identified and addressed the root cause of past rejections. Have you ever wondered why you may be prone to rejection? Is it a generational curse? Is it a learned behaviour? Could it be soul tie related? Are you rejected or are you the "rejecter" for lack of a better term?

Confusion, fear and rejection including other factors can imprison you for life if you do not identify them early enough to deal with them. You can become your own worst enemy and alienate yourself from experiencing real love. I am not a love guru nor am I an expert on love, however, my own personal love-dentity experiences afforded me to discover ways to accept and embrace reconditioning my mind-set. I acknowledged that if I did nothing about my love-dentity crisis, no one else could rescue me from it. I had to accept my wrongs and work on my imperfections before it was too late.

I derived an M.O.T analogy and named it the "M.O.T Love Test." An M.O.T is a UK compulsory annual test for safety and exhaust emissions of motor vehicles of more than a specified age. If your vehicle fails this test, it is deemed unsafe on the road. Therefore, you need to get the failed parts or components fixed, changed or serviced in order for your vehicle to be deemed safe again after a retest. Your heart has been around for a number of years now, and it has been moved or played up and down like a "yo-yo" toy several times.

I would assume that there has been some form of damage or wear and tear to it. This makes it qualify for a safety test so that any problems found can be addressed accordingly. Furthermore, I think that you and I need to do regular M.O.Ts to check the status of our hearts. Whether you are a believer of the word not, I hope this test will provide a unique insight to your love-dentity crisis.

The M.O.T. Love Test adapted from 1 Corinthians 13 vs 4-8 (NIV):

Love is patient, love is kind. It does not envy, it does not boast, it is not proud.

It does not dishonor others, it is not self-seeking, it is not easily angered, and it keeps no record of wrongs.

Love does not delight in evil, but rejoices with the truth.

It always protects, always trusts, always hopes, and always perseveres.

Love never fails. But where there are prophecies, they will cease; where there are tongues, they will be stilled; where there is knowledge, it will pass away.

Replace every **love** or **it** word with your name to personalize it. Do you now recognize where you are in terms of love? Are you patient or kind? Do you always rejoice with truth and keep no record of wrongs? Do you always protect those around you? Do you defend them in their absence?

This M.O.T Love Test is one of many things that can help you unlock your love-dentity crisis. Until you can master this test, you will continue to struggle with love and struggle in love. Rome was not built in a day, henceforth mastering this love test may take you a while. The key is in taking the difficult first step. Get on your max, get ready, steady and go work on any love-dentity crisis that you have identified. Once you set off, the rest will follow. When you fall, do not be afraid to get up and start again. Only a fool will think that it's a waste of time to start over.

I have a love-dentity story that I would like to share with you. This is a real letter that a friend of mine wrote to someone she was intimately involved with. She gave me full permission to share her letter with you. Hopefully, you can a learn thing or two from her love-dentity crisis.

Dear John (not his real name)

You claim you never want to leave things in life hanging yet you clearly do. Help me understand why you contradict what you say at times? This is not the first. I've been trying to make sense out of day one you claimed to be crazy about me, till now, where you're treating me like shit. Like I don't deserve to be loved or cared for.

I may not be the greatest person at relationships coz I got into this one unexpectedly and after a really long time. But one thing I know for sure is I am not a fool, as you'd like to believe not to be one yourself as well. Hence the reason I value communication so much and have emphasized on that so many times. Time for my closure and genuinely never want to leave things in life hanging. Keep in mind that this is not to attack you, but to make you see through a different lens, which I noticed you find difficult doing, believe it or not.

You're not as perfect as you want to portray yourself to be in relationships, the same way I'm not either. The difference is I'm not like your other girls that you claim come back looking for you after you've manipulated them to think that you're the best thing that ever happened to them because I understand it takes two to tango. A part of them once meant something to you till you were done with them only for you to dispose of them.

Yes, you can be a loving person if you want to, but you can really push someone over the edge which might overshadow the best in you. I'm not here to tell you who you are because you already know yourself or to justify my actions in response to your treatment towards me, but to tell you my own experience with you from day one and seek answers if you're kind enough to give them to me. I stand to be corrected if need be because some of it could be biased through assumptions based on how you've pushed me to shutting myself, and get back to protecting myself as usual.

So you told me how you felt about the ultimatum of picking between me and smoking (after lying to me, one of my deal breakers, which led me to doing that). And went on to tell me that I was bullying you, which I failed to understand how that so, yet you're the one that had lied and began to do it in my face and kissing me after the fact.

I understand when bullies identify the next person as they are, it's because they've been called out on their "BS" and the only way they can protect themselves is by calling the next person exactly what they see themselves as. I'm not going to get into that because I'd like to believe that we had spoken about it, and closed that chapter Thursday night. But to my surprise, on Friday you went on to treat me like shit.

Now let me begin by asking what you really want from me, or what your intentions were for starters? I'm so confused. You talk about unfairness yet you can't seem to see your bit of it by playing with someone's emotions and confuse the hell out them. Since you said you'd not smoke in front of me, I assumed that you meant for us to keep going.

But, it looks like I may have assumed wrong and I should have asked for clarity. I wasn't even comfortable being touched by you that night till after we spoke about it and thought we were ok. If anything, I felt used for your sexual needs rather than being emotionally present and connected with each other that night only for you to be rude the next day, out of nowhere. I even said I love you that same night and the next day in the morning, but you literally ignored me. Now is that what you call being fair? Is that your mature way of doing relationships as an adult? Or would it be fair for me to judge you like every other men, let alone that you're still legally married and want to use women for their sexual needs lying in the name of love?

I'm not going to lie to you, I feel my worst nightmare has come to life. You asked me what my fears were and I told you one of them. Now I feel like you're intentionally doing that to hurt me and thank you so much for it because time

13

heals. What hurts the most though is that I'm going back to square one of healing from such pain.

I understand there's what they call the honeymoon phase of relationships, but I did not think it would turn this ugly so soon. I wish I had backed off the moment I felt like doing it, but you manipulated me to think of why you fell in love with me. I chose to do it differently this time around and not just walk away without even trying. I'm not like you who thinks the more you get hurt the more it doesn't hurt so much.

Unfortunately, I'm the opposite that's why I took forever to get into a relationship. Let alone a relationship with so much baggage, baggage that I would have never compromised... knowing me. It took a lot for me to accept you the way you are, considering the influence around me. I am one not to judge people from gossip and I'm sure you've seen that. Actually this relationship taught me what compromising truly means. I think I told you from the word go that the sad thing about me is when I love, I love hard and it took me a while to open up my heart to you.

Heck, you even went into third person conversation asking how best you can win my heart and get me to love you back. I found that to be one of the most adorable things that got me giving you a chance. I think I've told you this and I'll tell you one last time that I'm the most authentic person you'll ever find. What you believe the rest of the world does or thinks or says or you've experienced is totally the opposite of who I am when I tell you who I am.

When I'm upset, you'll for sure know it because I'll show it to you. When I'm happy, that's no brainer. With that being said, you found me happy and didn't imagine for us to be where we're at today, but I'd appreciate if you'd left me the way you found me. Have you ever asked yourself why I'm not as happy as you found me, my usual norm? Have you ever gotten back to making a conscious effort to bring back that smile? I've been asking myself that question literally everyday (and in tears that I currently have no control over because of my treatment) since the day you started showing me your true colours.

I'm not going to lie to you I'm deeply hurt and not afraid to express it because I need the healing for myself. Like I said, I'm not like the rest of the world who'd think this to be absurd to do. Whether you read it or you don't, it's for my own good just releasing what's hurting me inside because I hate fighting with people anyway. By me telling you, it shows how much you meant to me, otherwise, you of all the people know that I usually just walk away with no words said.

It's so unfortunate that you found me in the middle of something that alters my mood which doesn't make our relationship any better, unless you really want to get back to putting an effort to it like you used to at the beginning. I've tried not to put the side effects of my medication on you or address that bit with you because of the positive mind-set I had maintained since I started my treatment, knowing the impact it might have on me.

Thank God, I have people who've been there since day one of my journey, who genuinely care about me coz they know me, and I was quite happy that I felt I had succeeded that bit of the journey without experiencing the other side effects. It took a lot for me to decide on whether or not I wanted to go on it. Heck, I had been celibate for years and had made a covenant with God on that.

I had never had unprotected sex in my life and had vowed not to indulge again into any sexual activity until it was with the right person and at the right time, after marriage. I compromised 80% of my values which led to my identity crisis that I could not even address to you because you didn't give me the room to do that. You're probably asking yourself what I mean by that. Yet you always said you want me to be myself, but the moment I tried to do that you'd shut me down. It became difficult for me to do that.

Right, let me take you back to when you acted as though you showed concern about my well-being each and every day if not every second. When you proclaimed your love for me, it felt so amazing. Heck that's one of the things that made me fall in love with you. What woman does not want attention and love, please tell me? Even the word on its own points out for men to be loving which automatically (with no doubt or request) allows the woman to be submissive and trust their significant other. I think the mistake I made was to give myself to you, let alone unprotected, leading to creating a spiritual bond and fornicating in the eyes of God.

I felt so convicted each and every day I did that. I have tried to live quite an obedient life, had prerequisites of entering into a relationship (one of them being getting tested). Argh, I'm tired of justifying who I am, you chose to judge me based on your experiences, but unwilling to get to know me personally; so basically it's a waste of time. You even went on to tell me that I have anger issues, wow, that is still a painful pill to swallow because I'm tired of literally swallowing them anyway.

You're the same person that told me that the reason you like me and want to be with me was the fact that I'm

16

genuinely joyful. Heck, you even said if you knew I was genuinely bubbly the way I am you wouldn't have bothered for us to be in a relationship because of your experience with people that hide their true misery under a fake joyfulness. You were even surprised by the way I was so positive the moment my car got stolen. Which now brings me to what contributed to my inner joy and how/when you found me.

Seems like you're forgetting that you found me trying to figure my stolen vehicle. Where was it stolen, at the gym right? Why did I go to the gym literally every day? Because of my treatment and we all know that working out is a natural anti-depressant. Heck I danced alone and enjoyed every bit of it while I was at the gym the same way I enjoy car karaoke, what beats such joy? Then you call me I'm an angry person. It's still a wow to me.

I do not disagree that I'm short tempered, but I intentionally choose not to let it out because I end up saying things that I'll regret and besides, I just hate that side of me so I'd rather keep quiet. You're even the first to tell me that I'm an angry person and definitely the last. I feel like not only did you push me on the edge to come off as that, but because you judged me based on what I've been through in my past contributed to your statement. I totally get it, and I don't blame you. But did I ever judge you based on your past? Correct me if I am wrong. I think I'm known to ask when in doubt.

But if I ever did, I'm truly sorry and for forgetting that. Then again now you've gotten me to shutting myself off again because I noticed that everything I say sounds so negative to you and it's weird how that changed. I appreciated the way you used to kindly give me a different

17

perspective to my opinions when you didn't agree with them. That felt like it came from a loving place. I believe a decent conversation allows everyone to have their opinions and if you do not agree with them ask for deeper understanding instead of coming off as though you know it all, like you're the only one that's experienced life.

People are so different, we come from different backgrounds and some of the things we can do in this world to show compassion and appreciation for one another is respect each other's opinions and ask for understanding when it doesn't resonate with our knowledge. Yes I may be way younger than you, but I'd like to believe that I have some bit of wisdom of my own too.

In this regard, I'll give you an example of the video I watched yesterday on red table talk. Actually I'll send it to you. You already know everyone be talking about white people privilege for the longest time. This young girl learnt to understand that the hard way, after not understanding it at all. Not that she was ignorant, but because of her surrounding which seemed to be normal to her.

Even after her parents got arrested for fraud (which involved her and her sister unaware) and using their white people privilege, she still didn't see it wrong why the world was bashing at her like that. She had to learn the lesson the hard way after brands retracted their partnership with her and began to lose followers.

Only then did she take time to learn and understand what white people privilege means and it has changed her mind-set leading to her growth. Now she advocates for people of colour and wants to use her platform to address that white people privilege is real. Moral of the story, background plays a role in how people think. Just coz you know what you know, don't expect the next person to know it the way you do.

I've even tried to say to you many times that don't judge me personally based on what you've experienced in you past relationships with the same statement that I might say. Never in my life have I said no you're wrong to think that way. The same way you wouldn't appreciate me bringing my past in our relationship which again I subconsciously did and didn't realize it, but understood after you pointed it out.

So this is all that's in my heart and felt the need to let it out and lastly ask why you're treating me like I'm some piece of shit. I don't deserve such treatment and if I'd known that's who you truly are I wouldn't have bothered responding to your hi, let alone accepting your proposal to take me to and from work when my car got stolen, the breakfasts and calls that came with it. I'm deeply hurt and thank you for all you've been. I respect people that do unto others as they'd like them to do unto you, which I believe would be an act of kindness.

But this, I just didn't expect it and I'm sorry, but I'm a different breed and cutting off communication would be what's best for me and my healing, and having you around is the worst thing for it. I hope this does not sound like bullying or unfair, just because I've expressed my feelings. Don't ever deprive me or anyone for that matter to express their feelings by categorizing them or calling them names for your own ego or personal gain or protection. That is outright emotional abuse if you ask me, but did I say that to you before? If you know you're not that person then don't take my word for it, but I've also had my own share of experiences.

Thank you for protecting and loving me when you did. I still love you, but if the feeling is not mutual I have to let you go because I'm not going to allow myself to get hurt any more than I already am. I've made a lot of poor choices in this relationship for the first time in my life and I understand that I made my bed, now it's time for me to lie in it and hope for good health after I get my blood works done, no pregnancy and a better tomorrow. Only God knows how to deal with me right now.

If the below does not resonate with us I think it's best and fair that we let each other go:

"Love is patient and kind. Love is not jealous or boastful or proud or rude. It does not demand its own way. It is not irritable, and it keeps no record of being wronged. It does not rejoice about injustice, but rejoices whenever the truth wins out. Love never gives up, never loses faith, is always hopeful, and endures through every circumstance."

1 Corinthians 13:4-7 NLT

So let me know.

Lastly, Love is a choice! Thank you for giving me the opportunity to love again after a long time. It was great while it lasted.

Tanya (not her real name)

Tanya and I had had several conversations about her past relationships and how they made her feel. She has trust issues and insecurity issues, and I have always been a shoulder to cry on several occasions. Irrespective of the advice and counselling given to stay away from some toxic situations, she was not mentally ready to let go. She hung on to them toxic-buggers and always had justified excuses for being with them. Tanya had always been afraid to face the man in the mirror until John happened. The pie is in the pudding – her letter to John.

When she called me in the middle of the night crying out the whole Indian Ocean, I knew I had one job to do this time – to listen only. I needed her to take full responsibility of her love-dentity crisis. It was time. She told me she had finally identified and accepted her issue, and she was ready to work on it. She was ready to break free. She was ready to let go, let God and live life in peace. She was ready to love herself first, and then maybe love again later.

It takes a lot of "balls" to accept the inevitable truth about your crisis and to walk away from it. However, when the time is right nothing can and nothing will stop you.

Someone close to my heart once reminded me of something very simple, but mind blowing. He said, "Shingie, love is a decision. Whatever you do in love, however you get to the crazy and beautiful moments, the sad and the good times, the crying and the rejoicing, the valleys and the mountains, the positive and the negative; just remember that love is a decision." You decide who to love and how to love them. You decide who loves you back and how much of their nonsense you can tolerate. It's all down to you.

So for those that are in long-term and committed relationships, including the already married ones, please remember that you decided to be readily available for "better or for worse." You decided to be in the position you are in right now. You decided to sign up for whatever you are complaining about or happy with. Yes you did not see it coming. However, now that it has arrived, you must deal with it.

If you are currently struggling with the decision you've made, ask yourself if your current position in- love right now makes any sense to you. Are you happy? Is there anything you can do to feel any better or different? Is there anything you can change? Who currently holds the keys to your love-dentity crisis? Is your heart in need of an M.O.T check?

As I grew older, and having gone through a few relationships and one or two flings, I eventually had to face my own confusion, rejection and fears. I had to admit that I am an imperfect being that can be hurt and hurt others too. We all make wrong choices and mistakes, but do we have to let them define us?

Learning from my mistakes, I made a decision to be in love with God first, to love myself and to love everyone as I ought to be loved. Besides, it is only wise to do unto others as you would like them to do unto you. I then understood that:

- Love does not control me; it allows me to be myself 24/7

- Love does not verbally, physically or mentally abuse me; it honours and cherishes me
- Love does not set professional, career or friendship boundaries; it allows me to freely grow
- Love does not discourage or demotivate; it encourages and motivates
- Love does not disable, it enables endlessly
- Love does not dictate the rules of life; it lets me live, learn, laugh and enjoy the love journey
- Love does not manage my social media, my emails, my phone; it trusts and respects
- Love does not suffocate me; it takes my breath away
- Love does not take me away from the presence of God because God is love
- Love loves

Dear you, do not give up on love and do not give up on yourself. Identify and work on your love-dentity crisis.

Remember when I mentioned, "For God does not give us the spirit of fear, but of power, love and a sound mind?" This means that you have the power to turn that fear into faith. Turn the confusion into composure. Turn the rejection into acceptance. All you need is the faith of a mustard seed. You have the power to turn every negative into a positive. The power to experience real love for the rest of your life journey. The power to stop painting everyone with the same brush.

The power to feel human again. The power to forgive and forget the trauma. The power to rebuild every broken wall. The power to mend broken hearts. The power to restore and reconcile. The power to tread upon every serpent set against you. The power to love with a sound mind. A mind that knows and recognises that you are fearfully and wonderfully made. You are that you are.

Let love praises rise from the inside of you.

Chapter 3

The Friends-dentity Crisis

Do not be afraid of being alone. Be afraid of having the wrong company around you. Certain people can pull you off the grid or influence you negatively if you are not careful. Having bad friends is worse than having no friends at all. Always analyse the motives of the ones you call your friends because only iron sharpens iron.

I think it is normal to want to have great friends around you all the time. To a certain extent, you want friends that will never let you down, never break your heart, never betray you, never lie to you, never use you, never manipulate you, and never take you for granted in any form or shape. In an ideal world, your friends are supposed to be there for you no matter what. They are supposed to laugh with you, cry with you, dance with you, pray with you, fight (for a good cause) with you, travel with you, and work in harmony with you. You need what they call a "ride or die," the day one kind of friends.

You need friends you can call anytime and they will drop everything to be there for you. Friends that can defend you in your absence, they don't judge you at all, but they appreciate you for who you are. The million dollar question is do such friends exist on this planet? Do you have such friends?

Jim Rohn once said, "You are the average of the five people you spent the most time with." This is a very common connotation that has defined a lot of friendships, including how others relate with their so called "acquaintances." It seemingly implies that you are an artefact of those you spend most of your time with. Some say that our closest friends greatly influence our lives in one way or another. They play a part in our way of thinking, our self-esteem and more importantly our decision making. However, I believe that the famous quote, "show me your friends and I will show you your future" echoes some debatable views because you cannot paint everyone with the same brush.

As an individual you could be surrounded by powerful, intelligent and ambitions people, but your energy will be the total opposite to theirs. Contrariwise, you could be the only one that is level headed in your circle of friends, and have no absolute impact on them. My own friendships to date have shown me that not every bad apple spoils the bunch, likewise, not every friend in need is a friend indeed. I have experienced the good, the better, the best, the bad, the toxic and the fake friendships.

I once had a friend whom I considered to be my own sister. We shared and did everything together until it all went south. I was so blinded by our friendship so much that I did not realise the spirit of jealousy and envy that was operating in her life. Linda (not her real name), worked as a housekeeper at a five star hotel in the city we both resided. I was a college student at the time, and I needed a part time job to be able to sustain my basic financial needs. I came across some housekeeping vacancies at the local hotel that Linda worked at. They were advertised in the local paper. I then applied for the job and put her name down under personal references since she already worked there, and not to mention she was like a sister to me. Surprisingly, I never heard back from the hotel for almost two months.

One day I bumped into a lady that knew both Linda and I on a bus going into town. She worked as an assistant manager at that particular hotel. She did not know me personally, however, she had heard about me and seen me in town with Linda on several occasions. We then randomly engaged into general conversation as we sat next to each other on the bus. When she eventually asked for my full name during our conversation, she mentioned that she had seen it shortlisted for an interview two months prior.

She then told me that her senior manager had inquired about my skills and experience from Linda. To my greatest surprise, Linda had completely denied our friendship, moreover, she had spoken negatively about me, and I can only presume that it put the interview panel off. She was one of their trusted employees and they had every reason to believe that she wouldn't to lie to them.

My heart was completely shattered upon hearing what felt like fake news from an outside source. I felt numb and lifeless simultaneously. I was confused and dumbstruck.

My conscience became void for what seemed like a lifetime. I did not want to believe the cards that she had laid on the table. I wasn't ready for it. I felt as if she was sharing some bizarre information that she had read from a popular gossip forum.

Needless to say she noticed my sad countenance, and she immediately apologised for dropping this uncalled for grenade on me. She also tried to comfort me. However at this point, it was one minute too late. I just simply thanked her for sharing. I got off the bus at the next stop and I walked home for the rest of the journey. It was at least a good one hour to get home on foot. However, I just wanted to walk and shake it all off.

To cut a long story short, I had just realised how oblivious I had been of our friendship all these years. I had ignored or rather missed all the red flags from Linda all along. I had made up excuses for her inexcusable behavior the entire time. I had allowed her to be a part of my life, even though this wasn't reciprocated. People who knew Linda before we became friends had previously approached and warned me about her. But I chose to ignore all the negative and bad stuff they claimed she had said about me. It was a hard one to swallow and digest because I loved my friend. I believed that she could never intentionally hurt me. I was obviously in denial. I had no one else, but myself to blame for this crisis.

This particular experience plus a few unmentioned others, was an eye opener to my friends-dentity crisis. She masked her persona so perfectly and she took advantage of the kindness I showered her with. All along, she was a wolf dressed in sheep's clothing and she really caught me off guard.

They say that there is nothing new under the sun. Jesus had twelve friends – his famous disciples. Amongst the twelve, he had an inner circle of three that were closer to him than the rest of the group. These three were Peter, James and John. He taught, modeled and equipped all of them for ministry. He ate with them. He walked and connected with them. He basically shared and spent most of his life with them up until he was betrayed by Judas, which led to his crucifixion. As if that wasn't enough, Peter had previously denied Jesus three times before the rooster crowed.

The moral of this short story is that some friends including your inner circle, will at some point deceive you, gossip about you, lie about you, stab you in the back, use you, abuse you, turn against you, or sell you out to your adversaries the same way Judas Iscariot did to Jesus. Friends come, and friends go. If you are not careful, you may end up being caught up in very toxic and manipulative friendships. They will come in the name of having your best interest at heart. However, their only agenda is to ride with you until they have gathered enough ammunition to fire against you when you least expect it. Their mission is to destroy you. They are like an enemy which comes to kill, steal and destroy. Stay woke!

Every group of friends is comprised of assorted personalities.

Some of these include the following:

The peacemakers – These are the ones that diffuse all the unnecessary drama. They have an anointed personality that is soothing, comforting and it makes you feel safe around them. They hardly entertain "noise" in their lives. They are warm, friendly and they always dispense and pour out positive vibes.

The gossipers – Nothing and I mean nothing gets past this type. They have files and archives on everyone. You'd think that they hold first class degrees or PhDs in gossiping. They love to waste your time by engaging in long tele-gossip conferences if you entertain them. The peculiar thing is that they have no side because they gossip with you, and they also gossip about you. They hardly have anything positive to say about you or others.

The attention seekers – These are annoyingly worse than needy teething babies. They crave attention so much that it can get under your skin. They want to be relevant and be acknowledged all the time. The will do whatever it takes to steal someone else's limelight. Attention seekers tend to be joy-killers because they inevitably dampen the mood with their sporadic behaviour. It is always about them and they don't consider anyone else's feelings.

The quiet ones – These hardly get involved in anything, and they always play it safe. They can spend a whole year without saying anything to anyone. The quiet ones can be very dangerous because you never know what they are thinking or when they will explode. However, a positive quality about them is that they know how to mind their own business.

The know it all – These ones can be irritating at times. They are also a bit controlling. Their energy is good and bad at the same time. They also tend to fake it till they make it. They come in very handy especially when you need an immediate solution to a complex situation. They may not always have sound advice, but they will somehow direct you in the right way.

The confidants – These are reliable and trustworthy. You can trust them to take your secrets to the grave. The confidants are keepers for life.

The influencers – Everyone needs one of these. They are full of life and positivity. They inspire and encourage you all the time. There is never a dull day with the influencers. They want to see you win with them and they tend to have your back.

The haters – These are self-explanatory. They are just simply pure haters and enemies of progress. They discourage you, and they carry and pass on negative energy 24/7. You can never please the haters. They want to see you suffer and lose whilst they pretend to be your pillar of support.

The liars – These ones take the friends-dentity award. They lie about anything and everything. I cannot even get into detail about the liars. I will let you think of, and digest all the liars you have come across.

The stingy ones – Lord have mercy! How do I even begin to describe these ones? I will make it plain and simple. They are just stingy with everything. They like to take, but do not like to give or share at all. Their true colours normally come out especially at celebrations or events were corporate input is required. They always bring out their calculators when it's time to settle the bill. For example, they tend to pay for only what they have consumed. Nothing more, nothing less as they count every penny.

The prayer warriors – There is always a dedicated spiritual one in the group. However, the prayer warriors are mostly teased because of their wild history. Yes, I happen to be one of them, and yes I had my wild moments back in the day. Yes, I fell a few times, but I got up, repented and refocused. Yes, I am imperfect, but I always try to be a better person each day. I am not ashamed to say so because I am that I am, and I have been through so much to be where I am today. However, I do thank God for salvation, grace, mercy and deliverance.

The interesting thing is that someone (the devil of course) is always trying to bring down or discourage the prayer warriors by reminding them of their past life. T.D Jakes once said, "My history is not my destiny. That's why I do not care when you say you knew me "when." Until you know me now, you don't know anything at all." To all my prayer warriors, please stay rooted and strong because the joy of the Lord is your strength.

Anyway, the prayer warriors tend to hold the group together by fighting spiritual warfare. They are always available in times of trouble in paradise, trials, convictions and tribulations. Their main job is to intercede at any given time and request. They also keep everyone spiritually motivated and encouraged. Where others need to have their faith boosted, need to be brave and courageous, need to stay strong and aligned, the prayer warriors are always there to extend a helping hand.

I could go on till the sun comes up about the different types of friends that are out there, but I will stop here. I think by now you have managed to identify the types of friends that you have.

*****

Have you ever hurt a friend or a group of friends unintentionally, but they thought differently about your actions? The answer is probably yes. You do certain things unknowingly with good intensions, but those intensions yield negative implications or they are misconstrued. Some friends will confront you about it, allow you to talk it out, reflect, reconcile the matter, forgive each other and mutually move on with life.

Some will distance themselves from you, completely block any form of contact without affording you the chance to redeem yourself. Some will simply avoid you whilst they carry the heavy burden in their hearts for life. Some will probably forgive you, but not forget, and will bring it up at any given opportunity when you have a disagreement or when there's an audience. Some will use it as a weapon to turn everyone else against you. The list of probabilities is endless.

If you have ever been hurt and you know exactly how it feels to be hurt, then you will understand why some of them will never want to associate with you for life. Please find comfort in knowing that this is absolutely normal. They are allowed to do as they wish because they have free will. Allow them to heal over time. Allow them to go through the process as they see fit. Forgive yourself for the pain you have caused, and forgive them for not accepting your apology.

Do not force them to understand what happened or how it happened. When the time is right, it will all work out as it should. Just let go and let God deal with their hearts, for He knows their heart's desires more than you ever will.

God will only forgive you if you first forgive all those you've inflicted pain on. Remember the Lord's Prayer? "Forgive our trespasses as we forgive those who trespass against us." Please do not shoot the messenger. Take this conversation up with God – thank you!

Do not force friendships because they seem ideal. Do not compromise your mental health, your dignity nor your persona just to be able to fit in. Do not be a friend of the world. The bible reminds us, "You adulterous people, don't you know that friendship with the world means enmity against God? Therefore, anyone who chooses to be a friend of the world becomes an enemy of God. You ought to evaluate every relation you have with your friends. Are they building you or are they destroying you?

Some friendships are a set up for your downfall. As you identify the types of friends you have, including the type of friend you are; you need to allow God to grant you the serenity to accept the things you cannot change. The courage to change the things you can, and the wisdom to know the difference. Learn to accept that not everyone you call a friend will do some of the following aspirant things:

- Like or welcome you with open arms
- Support all your goals and dreams
- Be honest, open, transparent or trustworthy
- Pray for you as you pray for them
- Encourage, motivate and inspire you
- Put your feelings and emotions into consideration

Nothing ever just happens by coincidence. There's always a reason for everything. Identify and work on your friends-dentity crisis. Be very watchful, and ask God to give you the wisdom and knowledge to be able to deal with issues that have been deterring you from moving from glory to glory.

As you evaluate, analyse and action your friends-dentity crisis, remember to forgive yourself, forgive them and move on. Love your enemies and pray for those that persecute you.

"We must keep moving, we must keep going. If you can't fly, run. If you can't run walk. If you can't walk, crawl, but by all means keep going" – **Martin Luther King**.

Chapter 4

The Career-dentity Crisis

"It is always hard along the way to what we want. We have to pour in a lot of work, endure a lot of pain and deal with fears and uncertainties" **– Unknown**.

O ur career paths are driven by various forces, goals, desires and circumstances. Some of these driving dynamics are favourable, whilst others are quite the opposite. You wrestle with a lot of economic pressure, social pressure, family pressure and peer pressure when deciding on which career to settle for. You know that unless you put your sweat and blood in it, someone else is out there doing it better than you. You are constantly in a career progression maze, but I wonder if you are chasing your desired goals, or if you are just living under someone else's career-dentity shadow?

Here are a few common questions to get you started on your career-dentity crisis:

- Do you like your career right now?
- Is your career in line with your university/college degree?

- Do you enjoy what you do or are you in it just for the money?
- Does your job pay handsomely or is it a hand to mouth arrangement?
- Do you wish you could venture into a different career?
- Is your age a limiting factor to start pursuing your dream career?
- Are you affected by education, economic and social status?
- Are you just a career-dentity victim due to pathological procrastination?

Some people have their careers chosen or lined up for them and some work hard to attain their desired careers. Some are not ambitious enough to pursue their goals, and some are just career procrastinators by nature. Some are so driven that they will travel millions of miles away from home, leaving their families and loved ones behind in pursuit of their careers. Their mind-set is focused on winning and putting food on the table. They do not believe in failure, and they are more than prepared to endure any risks and costs, as long as they strike the jackpot in the end. Some are fortunate enough to have the comfort of working from their home or anywhere in the world because they either own an online or virtual business. On the other hand, others find themselves involved in demoralising activities such as stealing, prostitution, or being involved in fraudulent and illegal business in order earn and sustain a living.

Some lose their jobs due to natural disasters or unexpected global pandemics that ferociously affect the economy such as the Covid-19 pandemic. The Covid-19 pandemic has by far had an unwarranted impact on a lot of careers. We have witnessed vast industries going into administration, hundreds to thousands of retrenchments, and business closures due to the tenacious loss of income and revenue. Unfortunately, this will be an ongoing matter possibly until the pandemic comes to a halt. Henceforth, some people are forced to settle for any jobs that they can find even though they may not be under favourable working conditions.

Contrariwise, it has also been a blessing in disguise to others. It has been that ray of sunshine on a cloudy day. Some have established businesses, whilst some invigorated opportunities, especially those running digital and virtual platforms. I have two very close friends of mine who managed to start an online business known as "The Sweet Sponge."

They custom make and sell splendid cake toppers for all occasions. Their online business has been on what they call a "bullish" trend in trading terms. The reconditioning of their career mind-set and determination came right in the middle of the first lockdown, and their business is portraying explosive signs of growth and success. This was all due to them identifying their career-dentity crisis because of the pandemic, and immediately taking the necessary action. Munya and Janet did not allow themselves to be incapacitated by the pandemic economic downfall. However, they chose to rise above the obstacle. They chose to be invincible.

What is your career-dentity story? Have you been affected in some way? It may not be the pandemic, but it could be other factors. What actions have you taken so far? Do you have a dormant business plan or idea that could change your life? What is stopping you from shooting your shot? Is fear stopping you? When are you going to wake up and smell the coffee?

*****

I always dreamt that I would be a very successful chartered accountant one day. I remember when I was in high school, my mother would hide my text books away from me because of the amount of home studying I did after school. At that time, I was doing my IGCSEs (International General Certificate of Secondary Education) at a private British school back in Botswana. My personal study routine consisted of putting in an extra five hours in the evening, on top of my normal school timetable.

During the weekends, I would lock myself in my room and study my favourite subject - accounting until mum came to take away and hide my books so that I could get a break from them. I enjoyed studying the subject so much that I would miss meals and not feel hungry. If you know my love relationship with food, then you will definitely understand how much accounting meant to me at the time.

Nonetheless, just before I sat for my IGCSEs, I managed to secure a conditional internship with a reputable financial services firm called PricewaterhouseCoopers. I had no intention of going to university because my mother couldn't afford it at the time. She was a single mother who had a lot of mouths to feed and look after; nine siblings and other extended family. Moreover, I had already convinced myself that I was not cut out for university.

The contractual agreement was that PricewaterhouseCoopers would invest in me through full time training, and provide a bursary for three years until I became qualified. Afterwards, they would be inclined to offer me a full time position based on my skills and performance. I was over the moon about my future career since it was my dream job. I had found a way to kick start my CA career. I worked even harder at school so that I could do exceptionally well in my final exams. The conditions were to pass Accounting, Mathematics and English with at least a B grade respectively.

Fast forward to two months after I secured the internship, some distant uncle decided to convince my mother that I was better off in the IT industry compared to the financial industry. My mum was naively persuaded and that was the beginning of an end to my CA career. You can imagine exactly how I felt about such news. I was completely devastated and disappointed that someone would intervene with my future plans. I honestly felt as if this particular uncle had been sent by the devil himself. Have you ever had that one person that comes to kill, steal and destroy your plans? For me, it was this particular uncle. I really disliked him for a while until I found Jesus. I forgave him, but I have clearly not forgotten.

I did not like IT nor did I want to work in the IT industry. I saw myself as a happy and successful CA. To cut a long story short, my dreams were completely shattered and I found myself at an IT college after I passed my IGCSEs. I hated it, however, I still had to do it. The fact is I wasn't funding the course myself due to obvious reasons; I was an unemployed fresh off high school with no money dependant. This meant I had to do as I was told. It was either IT or nothing. Those were the painful parameters. At this point, I had a career-dentity crisis.

I continued to study IT two years on when I moved to England to further my studies. Just to add salt to injury, I was the only female in a class of fourteen. This caused a bit of discomfort and discouragement, moreover, it fuelled my distaste for the IT career. Do not get me wrong because IT is such a great and fast moving industry with rewarding remuneration. Moreover, most jobs now heavily rely on virtual technology. It is just not my cup of tea no matter how much money is involved. I have zero passion for it.

You may be wondering if I eventually pursed my dream CA career at some point in life. Unfortunately I did not. I cultivated so much resentment towards my uncle that I also fell out of love with my dream career. It's a hard one to chew and I have no words to properly explain it. However, I convince myself that the trauma I went through my dream career getting shattered at such a young age, somehow destroyed any passion and confidence for pursuing it.

Upon reflection, I do have myself to blame for not pursing the CA career when I was now independent and able to make personal decisions about my life. I told myself that it was too late to chase that dream. There was no way I could revive the same energy that I had back then. My mum tried to push me back into it, but to no avail. The ship had long sailed.

Do you feel like you have been or are in a similar situation? You failed to pursue a dream career because it was prematurely shattered by someone else? Or you have had countless rejections or misfortunes from your chosen career, that you decided to pursue a different avenue? Have you been side-lined all the time there is a promotion at your work place, even though you work your socks off?

What next?

"Formal education will make you a living; self-education will make you a fortune. Don't wish it were easier. Wish you were better" – **Jim Rohn**

They say "knowledge is power". However, I strongly think that applied knowledge is power. I say so because you can be an educated fool and be very poor. This is simply because you may have a wealth of knowledge, resources and skills, but fail to utilise them effectively. This attests the aforementioned. There are a lot of people out there with degrees displayed on their walls symbolising the elephant in the room. However, if you apply the knowledge and skills (talents) accordingly, with a hint of bursting passion, you could make a dollar out of 15 cents.

If you want to be powerful and successful, you need to educate yourself. Educate yourself in the area you are very passionate and really give a toss about. It could be culinary, coaching, counselling, singing, painting, and the list is endless. If it is a gift, you should immensely invest in it and explore how you can turn it into a paying career. I repeat, you should immensely invest in it. I believe that a nurtured gift will always make room for you. Use your voice, use your hands, use your knowledge and skills, and use your talents to make it happen. Unless you take the risk, you are risking and lessening the chances of your success in having the career of your dreams.

The pursuit of happiness is coherently influenced by life accomplishments and achievements. But how does one get to achieve all they wish for or want? How does one shy away from a career-dentity crisis? How do you stop asking questions like:

- So what is the best career out there?
- Am I free to choose a career I want without letting my parents down?
- Will my partner approve of the next career path I want to purse?
- What will my family and friends think of me as a full time musician or make-up artist?

43

- I do not have any capital, how will I start?
- The market is already flooded, how will I break through?
- Will people follow, like and support me?
- Am I good enough and will I get the respect I deserve?

Firstly, you ought to take time out to think. Take time to figure out how to engage with your inner self. Take time to go back to the drawing board when doubt suddenly creeps in. Take time to have the "hard talk" with yourself. For example, do you like waking up every day for that 9am to 5pm, Monday to Friday and sometimes Saturday or Sunday job? Do you enjoy the long commute to and from your workplace? Do you like your work colleagues, do you like your manager, and more importantly, are you happy with your current position? If the answer is NO (aka Next Opportunity), then what is your next step?

Where there is a will, there is always a starting point. I had to build radical habits that prevent distractions in order for me to stay focused on my character and career building. I had to avoid chasing the wind and start planting the right seeds because as the saying goes, "You reap what you sow." I did not want to reap disappointment, frustration, non-accomplishment, poverty and definitely not reap another career-dentity crisis.

Do not rush to sign up for any business ventures or investments without getting an in-depth knowledge of the strategies and the binding policies. If you ever watched

The Pursuit of Happyness by Will Smith, you will know exactly what I am talking about. If you haven't watched it, it's a must watch. He obliviously invested in a business plan that got him into serious debt. He ended up financially constrained that he was struggling to cater for some basic needs such as food, shelter and clothing. He chose a career which looked instantly lucrative, the get rich quick investments that most of us tend to fall for. For example, the popular Ponzi or pyramid schemes. I believe that lack of appropriate research about the market he had entered into soon became apparent.

However, as soon as he realised his career-dentity crisis, he reconditioned his mind-set. He re-directed his knowledge and skills to pursue the career that he had always wanted. It was not easy as he faced a lot of turbulences on the way, but it was worth it. He signed up for a six months unpaid stock broker internship with a reputable Wall Street investment company. In between his internship and studies, he still had to look after his son as a single dad. He had to sleep in unpleasant places for a while and still maintain his sanity and dignity. It got so bad one day that he even slept in a public toilet with his son. However, he still turned up for the unpaid internship the next day.

He had a vision, a goal to achieve and nothing was about to stop him from achieving it. He was so determined that he became the best student out of the entire class. He did not let his unfavourable circumstances determine his future. He did not allow anything to hinder his passion and progression. He was ready to win the war with the limited armour he had. He knew exactly what he wanted and he kept his eyes on the ball.

Therefore, do not let fear cripple your ambitions. Do not let someone else's opinion impede your pursuit for what you are called to do or what you are passionate about. Do not let the current pandemic or any other unforeseeable pandemic limit your horizons. Do not let past failures deter you from trying again. Do not let your current qualifications limit how far you can climb the career path ladder. Do not let them tell you that it cannot be done or achieved. Do not let society continue to flood your mind with negative and discouraging feedback. Do not keep letting yourself down. Anything is possible if you really put your mind to it. The question is, "How desperate are you for a complete turnaround of your career-dentity crisis?"

Again, please refrain from being concerned about other people's perceptions concerning your chosen career. If it didn't work for them, it does not mean that it won't work for you. Besides, one man's meat is another man's poison. Some love marmite and some absolutely hate it. Nonetheless, those that hate it do not affect its production. The market will still cater for those that love it. Your skills and talents will always have a place in the world no matter how competitive the career industry may seem.

Where there is a will, there is a way. Do whatever it takes to identify the what, why, when, where and the how. When I studied pharmacy at university, I learnt a very useful mnemonic that I have since applied to everyday critical situations. This mnemonic is often used by pharmacy professionals to gather information to help them in diagnosing a patient's presenting complaints and it's called the *WWHAM* questions.

(W) Who is the patient?

As obvious as this may sound, are you aware that you are the subject in this career-dentity crisis?

(W) What are the symptoms?

What are the obstinate things stopping you from progressing or identifying which career path to take?

(H) How long have the symptoms been present?

How long have you been procrastinating or contemplating on this career-dentity crisis?

(A) Action taken?

Have you attempted to sort it out or put any effort into fixing the crisis? Do you have a vision board?

(M) Medication being taken?

What steps have you put in place so far in order to shift the paradigm?

Take some time out to WWHAM yourself, reflect accordingly, and be clear and specific about your next career move.

Chapter 5

The Money-dentity Crisis

"Money is a concept. The concept of money comes with a lot of baggage to most of us. We have an inherent belief that it is good or bad and that wanting it is good or bad. That loving it is good or bad. That spending it is good or bad. There is no greater truth than this – money doesn't discriminate. It doesn't care what colour or race you are, what class you are, what your parents did, or even who you think you are. You have the same rights and opportunities as everyone else to take as much as you want" – **Richard Templar**

We all have the same 24 hours in a day, 365 days in a year to make money, and how you make that money is entirely your responsibility. How you make that money can either make you or break you. How you make that money can either weaken or strengthen you. How you make that money can bring forth sorrow or happiness. How you make that money can either build you or destroy you. How you that make that money can increase your enemies or increase good relations.

Money can get you places, and at the same time, the lack of money can make you miss out on a lot of "good" things in life. Money defines you because it affects how you make decisions, how you manage yourself, and those you are responsible for. Money can be your best friend or it can be your worst enemy – more money, more problems. Therefore, you have to be accountable for your actions and be able to live with the decisions you make.

We are all fearfully and wonderfully made, and so is money as it carries a certain prestige. A prestige that will either exalt you or humble you. Do people fear you when you have or do not have money? Do you feel wonderful around your minted (rich) colleagues, family or friends if you are the only "broke" one? Do you earn the same kind of respect with money compared to without money? What is it about money that creates love or hate, generosity or greediness, good or evil, anti-corruption or corruption, and all other miscellaneous things you can think of?

Money affects men and women differently, as it affects you and I differently. Money does weird and wonderful things for men especially the "ugly" looking ones. They have an attractive glow that comes with having a lot of money. Moreover, it brings power, it draws all kinds of women and it brings about fame. Money does somewhat the same for women, but with an interesting twist. It definitely brings power, independence, fame and the inverse; it attracts a lot of broke men. It also attracts a lot of lazy, lying and cheating vultures. It attracts some problematic "ben 10s" (a term commonly used for younger men by cougars). These are easy to control and manipulate as money is used as bait. It also attracts a lot of fake friends, and to a certain extent, it promotes a very materialistic lifestyle.

Money is a lot of things including causing mayhem. They say that the love of money is the root of all evil. Some people love money, but they aren't necessarily evil. However, some do love money to the extent of performing money rituals in order to obtain it. The love of money connected to evilness has to some extent been wrongfully attached to wealthy people especially within the Afro-Caribbean culture. If you are rich or wealthy, you are considered to have accumulated your money through some witchery or wizardry.

Some are accused of sacrificing human blood of their very own close family, or having cultic ornaments or reptiles that produce the money for them. This may sound absurd, however, when we search deeper into some biblical context, we find that 1 Timothy 6:10 states, "the love of money is the root of all evil." This denotes that money itself is not evil, but the love of it, is described as the root of all evil. It is therefore vital to understand what a money-dentity crisis can lead one into.

 King Solomon understood the rules of wealth. "A feast is made for laughter, wine makes life merry, and money is the answer for everything." Ecclesiastes 10:19. This means that money answers all, not some, but all things. In real life, it solves most of our problems or issues, but not all because we are just impossible to please. We need money for basic things like food, shelter, clothing, and survival. Without money, life will be inevitably challenging. I have had a few money-dentity crisis seasons. They came in different forms of shapes and sizes. Some were bigger than the others, some were more challenging and some were just unbearable.

Here goes...

There is a point in my life when I had a million plus questions because I had no cent to my name. I really struggled to make ends meet. Moreover, the stress and anxiety that came with poverty made it worse and very difficult to face each day. Sometimes I wished I was still an infant, heavily dependent on my mother for anything and everything. This would eradicate the need to worry about facing bills at the end of every month.

Have you ever sat down and calculated all your expenses versus your monthly income? If there is more going out versus what is coming in, then you may have experienced or you do suffer from high blood pressure, and some form of money related depression. I used to get extreme palpitations just thinking about the rent, council tax, car insurance, road tax, utilities, credit card repayments, mobile phone, Wi-Fi, TV-licence, fuel and the list goes on.

The irony is that I stupidly accumulated a money-dentity crisis in my life. My justified excuse is that I was young and naïve. I used to be so addicted to shoes that I would buy at least two to three pairs each month without fail. I didn't need all the shoes I bought back then. But the spirit of addiction and poverty had a massive stronghold on me. At the time this shoe addiction was in its infantry stages, I hardly had any bills to pay because I lived with my mum.

As aforementioned, I was young, reckless and naïve. It was only after I moved out of my mother's house and rented my own place, that I realised all the bad money decisions I had made all these years. I could have easily saved up, but I thought having the trending shoes then was more important.

I also made a lot of mistakes when I was at university. I used to have a part time job where I would get enough money to cover my rent, utilities, and still have some extra for groceries, toiletries and a tiny bit more towards my impulse spending. I also used to receive a university grant and a pharmacy bursary on top of my monthly income from my part time job. Life was definitely sweet and I lived like I had already made it in life.

When I look back at the money I received and wasted throughout my university life, I could have made some investments and savings that could have changed my life today. This was a money-dentity crisis that I didn't see coming. I wanted to look rich instead of thriving and working hard to be successful. I recklessly spent on liabilities instead of investing in stocks and assets or even just save up for a rainy day.

The sad truth is that our generation lacks financial literacy and so did I back then. We are taught to prepare for a 9am to 5pm job after we secure that degree. We are not financially diverse enough to understand the power of multiple streams of income. We exchange our time and energy each week to our employers. We work hard whilst others work smart. We work for our money till retirement whilst others let money work for them. If you are at a stage where you are not making money whilst you are sleeping, I am sorry to be the one to tell you that you still have quite a long way to go.

You, my friend, have a money-dentity crisis no matter how much your job pays you because anything can happen. You could get fired or retrenched. If you haven't expanded or utilised your skills elsewhere to earn some extra income, then it is time to do some serious reflection and do something about it. Sometimes we have to take a closer look at our abilities and capabilities when it comes to handling money. How do you manage your money? Are you the accountable and responsible type or are you the spoilt irresponsible brat? You need to check yourself and see why you have a money-dentity crisis.

I have often wondered if it is just me or if there is a ruthless spirit around supporting our own friend's or family's businesses? There seems to be a spirit of envy combined with jealousy that arises from a very unpleasant mind-set. A spirit that does not want to see others do better and make it in life. Unfortunately, this spirit dominates a lot within the Afro-Caribbean societies. I have seen more Asians and white people support one another more than the black man does with his own blood. There are some few exceptions so please do not catch artificial feelings over this statement.

Anyway, I wish I knew why we let this bad spirit deter our progression collectively as they say, "One can chase a thousand, but two can chase ten thousand." I will let you ponder on this one as you think of your own circumstances. Some of your own close people will claim that they are praying for your well-being, praying for your success and even encouraging you to go for it, yet they do not even raise a single finger to help, promote or support your business. This ill-wishing spirit is another form of money-dentity crisis. It almost feels like you keep hitting a brick wall every time you are about to have a financial breakthrough.

I have an acquaintance who comes from a very wealthy family, however, she seemed to be the only one in her family who struggled to make ends meet. She is very talented and passionate about her gift – cooking. She has some amazing culinary skills, however, her own family and some close friends wouldn't support her financially. They preferred to spend their money on alcohol, shopping, and going out or doing other things, except helping her with a start-up capital. She had a brilliant concept, but no money to fund it. It went on like this for years. This was her money-dentity crisis. In order to make some money, she needed some money, but she just couldn't make a financial breakthrough.

She shared is a list of some questions that used to run through her mind during her dark days:

- Why is getting money a struggle?
- How do I get money with less suffering?
- Where do I even start?
- Where is everyone else getting money from and how are they doing it?

- What platforms do I need to be a part of in order to get life changing money advice?
- What other project(s) can I venture into in order to start earning some real money?
- They say that money attracts money, so do I need to surround myself with wealthy people?
- Am I financially cursed?
- Do I have the generational poverty spirit attached to me?
- It is too late for me to start making money?
- Should I start gambling (playing the lotto) since they say you got to be in it to win it?

So what would you do in a situation like this? Do you just give up on your dreams because people you expect to help you do not help? Do you risk getting into debt by borrowing a loan from a bank or a loan shark in order to get started?

Everyone's hustle is different. If you are to build a house, you first have to have an idea of the type of house you want. You have to get a building plan, know the area where you plan to build. After the building plans are approved, you then begin the construction process by sourcing out building materials and the best builders for the job. You have to sort construction insurance to cater for unplanned disaster.

A strong house needs a solid foundation, followed by brick laying, one by one until you get to the roof. If it means starting your hustle off by offering free services for marketing purposes in order to get your name out there, then so be it. If you have to sell some of your belongings such as shoes, clothes or gadgets that you can do without, then just do it. You have to do what it takes to get started. I do not mean get involved in illegal activities please. Remember you reap what you sow. Therefore, if you sow incriminating seed, you have to endure the inevitable consequences.

Eventually, my friend decided that enough was enough. The struggle was real as she kept seeing all her friends and family enjoying financial freedom. No one was prepared to share the secrets to their financial success. She decided to take the risk and she applied for a bank loan. The rest is history as she's now the owner of a very successful restaurant. She did not let her money-dentity crisis hold her down forever.

One of my favourite money-dentity crisis example is a very profound story about the parable of the talents. A rich man gave his three slaves an amount of money (talents), according to each one's ability to steward, and to manage the money before he left the city. One slave was given five talents, another two talents and the last one was given only one talent respectively. The three slaves were entrusted to care for the talents in their master's absentia. The slave with five talents and the other with two talents both invested and doubled their talents to ten and four talents respectively. However, the slave with only one talent dug up a hole and buried the talent until their master returned from his trip.

The two slaves that had doubled the talents were rewarded handsomely by being put in charge of many things, whilst the slave who did nothing with his talent had it taken away from him. This was a result of irresponsibility, lack of wisdom, knowledge and understanding of the common rule of thumb, "you reap what you sow." The moral of the story is that you can only blame yourself for mishandling money. If you do not take charge to be responsible, accountable, faithful, loyal and trustworthy with your money matters, you will never come out of the poverty bracket. You will always have holes in your pocket and live a very frustrating hand to mouth type of life.

The first time I learned of this parable I was slightly taken aback. I never really thought that sowing had a correlating reaping effect. I started to pay more attention to how I handled my money and some of the bad money decisions I had made in my younger days. The bad decisions definitely yielded painful consequences, and I am not ashamed to say that I learnt the hard way. Have you ever avoided opening some of your mail because you knew by the colour of the envelope or the print on the address label that it was from the debt collectors?

I bet some of you are in that debt-collectors boat this very moment. You receive final warnings, but you still ignore them until you get a county court justice (CCJ) that will mess up your credit rating for a few good years. Like the slave with the one talent that was taken away from him, you have a lot of financial abilities and opportunities taken away from you until you fix your credit score, and until that CCJ is taken off your record. It is a hard one to swallow, but once you endure the disadvantages and hardships associated with carelessness, you will hopefully try and unlock the money-dentity crisis for the better.

They say you that learn something new every day. I can attest to this as I am still finding my feet each day. I have learnt and I am still learning to be more accountable and responsible with my finances. It may take a while to get to where you really want to be and to have that financial freedom. However, the important thing is to take the first step on the financial- ladder and believe in yourself. As you take each step, make sure that you are very careful until you get to the top of the ladder. Make sure you do it your own way, follow steps and procedures that are flexible and comfortable for you. Do not be pressured into creating another money-dentity crisis whilst trying to fix the one(s) you currently have. Do what you can, how you can and when you can. You can still learn from others, but please design your own template to follow through. Be inspired but do not copy.

Avoid the fake expensive life, avoid pleasing others when you cannot afford it. Avoid the expensive temptations and habits. Avoid peer pressure, avoid family pressure, avoid work pressure, avoid fashion pressure, and definitely avoid social-media pressure. Some of you have invested in things with little or no knowledge at all and therefore ended up losing everything. It is ok to say no because only you can get yourself out of that money-dentity situation. You can either work for money or have money work for you.

Are your money decisions assets or liabilities? Do you want to own a house or properties one day or do you want to keep renting, borrowing and asking others for help for the rest of your life? The decision is solely yours.

So how do you unlock this money-dentity crisis? There is no standard operating procedure as each money-dentity crisis is different. I have to put in a disclaimer that I am not a financial adviser, but I can tell you that unlocking this money-dentity crisis all begins with a changed mind-set. This is just free general knowledge that you need to embrace and implement. You have to admit to having a crisis and be willing to conform to positive change. You need to have a millionaire's mind-set and stop limiting yourself. You can do absolutely anything that you put your mind to, and you can do all things through Christ who strengthens you.

Some basic measures include looking at your spending habits. Make sure that you have more money coming in than you have going out each day, month and year. Check your monthly income vs expenditure in order to work out a feasible target. If your salary is not enough to make ends meet then maybe it is time to have multiple streams of income. How you decide which streams to take on depends on your gifts, talents, expertise and time you are willing to make it work.

1. Do you think it's time to be courageous enough to monetise your skills?

2. Is it time to do some extra research or training so that you are fully knowledgeable and equipped for the crypto-currency, stocks and forex trading platforms?
3. Do you think it's time to quite your full-time job and be your own boss?
4. Do you think it's time to go out and look for clients for that stagnant business?
5. Do you think it's time to set up that website that you have been meaning to finalise?
6. Do you think it's time to say enough is enough and just do it?

It is your money-dentity crisis, your decision – the ball is in your court. Get rich or die trying.

Chapter 6

The Tongue-dentity Crisis

"The *words* you speak identify you. The *words* you speak set the boundaries of your life. The *words* you speak affect your spirit. If you want to locate yourself, just listen to the *words* you speak" – **Kenneth E. Hagin**

The tongue is the most powerful tool that you possess. It has the supernatural ability to galvanise or disable life. In the first chapter of Genesis, it is written that God created the world through His spoken word. Genesis 1:3; "And God said, Let there be light: and there was light." In verse 11 God said, "Let the waters under the heaven be gathered unto one place and let the dry land appear: and it was so." These scriptures demonstrate the power of the spoken word. We are all created in God's image and therefore we have the authority to speak things into existence or non-existence.

Words are sharper than any two-edged sword. They can pierce through your heart, soul and spirit. Words can break or make you. Words can heal you or make you sick. Words can discourage or encourage you. Words can demotivate or motivate you. Words can close doors or open doors for you. Words can destroy or build you. Words can contaminate or purify you. Words can oppress or boost you. They can also bring doubt or cultivate faith in your life. The list is endless. Take note that the words you release at day break can have a negative or positive impact on the rest of your day. You can either kill, steal or destroy your destiny just by the words that come out of your mouth. Therefore, you need to be very careful of what you wish for because you might just get it.

My spiritual mentor often said to me, "As a man thinks in his heart, so is he and out of the abundance of the heart, the mouth speaks." I often took it lightly until I started to pay a bit more attention to what was happening around me. It felt surreal. Every thought I entertained and spoke literally came to fruition, be it good or bad. I soon realised that whatever baggage or treasure I carried in my heart consciously or subconsciously, somehow identified me, and it had a huge impact on my day to day life transitorily as I spoke it out.

Many a times, you do not pay close attention to the words that come out of your mouth. You obliviously release words that inevitably come to life because you speak them with so much subconscious confidence. These words are mostly released through what you may deem innocent or generic conversations that you have with your work colleagues, your friends and family and even with strangers. You think you are just having banter or casual dialog, however, every spoken word has power to manifest as you declare it.

Here are some of the common negative connotations you bring to fruition reluctantly:

- "Is this normal or am I rushing into things" (disbelief)
- "I am bored"
- "I will never make it"
- "I am poor"
- "I know I have been praying, but is this really from God because it is too good to be true" (disbelief)
- "Today is going to be such a tough and long day"
- "I am about to make the wrong decision, but what else can I do?"
- "I just don't have enough time to do all I want to do in a day"
- "This is a bad idea, but oh well"
- "I am such a failure"
- "I am such a disappointment"
- "I am not going to pass this exam/test; I can just feel it"
- "I am going for the interview, but I am not sure if I'm good enough for the position"
- "I can't do it no matter how much I try" (not believing in yourself)
- "I give up" (this happens usually before you even attempt it)
- "I am not well" (usually a white lie used to avoid going to work and then you actually end up feeling unwell)

Dear you, how you call it is exactly how it will be. As long as you keep calling things like they are, as long as you keep telling it like it is, those things are never going to change unless you reverse it. When negative words are released and planted like a seed against you, whether by you or by someone else and you take no action to rebuke them; they will manifest accordingly, and grow to negatively affect your life.

You therefore need to start paying more attention to what you or others say about you. You have to revamp the thoughts that you entertain prior to verbalising them. In most cases, once they are released out of an intense and emotional argument, it may be a little late to take it all back. Henceforth, the words manifest just as they were called out.

As I matured in mind, body and spirit, I started to be very careful about the things I spoke over my life. I had to learn how to think first before I uttered anything out. I learnt how to be quick to hear, and be quick to think, but slow to speak. Matthew 7:7 says that, "Ask and you shall receive." This means that you have to speak out whatever it is that you expect God to deliver you from or bless you with. Unless you do as it says, the idea or the unspoken word will just remain stagnant.

No one is perfect and we all make mistakes. We all curse sometimes (not good) especially when we are angry, frustrated, provoked or unhappy about something. We all ill-wish others when they have hurt us or have done us wrong. We say what we say in the spare of the moment. Sometimes we mean it and sometimes we don't. However, once we utter those words; positive or negative, we can't retract it. We have all wished someone dead because of how they mistreated us. The words we speak are very powerful, be it good or bad. We have eyes yet we do not see, we have ears yet we do not hear. The spiritual blindness and deafness makes us insensitive to how we label others. This is a very common form of tongue-dentity crisis.

You could be holding onto some toxic words that were spoken over your life by a family member, partner, work colleague, friend or an ex. You may have grudgingly let those words define or shape your life. You may lack confidence or suffer from very low self-esteem just because of how someone verbally or emotionally abused you. You may have been bullied a lot at school, called all sorts of names that affected your mental health, and how you relate to your surroundings. You may also suffer from cultural oppression that does not afford you the freedom to fully express your emotions.

If you decide to speak up you are either labelled as disrespectful or very rude. You are constantly reminded, "I am the father or the mother of this house, "I carried you for nine months, therefore, you must listen to everything I say because you owe me your life, "I pay the bills in this house, and therefore you have no input whatsoever, "Do you know how I much I suffered and what I went through to give you a better life than I had?"

The list of these negative and manipulative threats are over the top. Unfortunately, these threats are contributing factors to how you may identify yourself, and what you may speak over your life. By default, your tongue adopts these conditioned beliefs and limiting perceptions.

Take a minute to think about this. If something is embedded in you over a long period especially from childhood to your early adult years, it may become a perpetual stronghold that will deem extremely impossible to just instantaneously shake off. Every time your voice is silenced, you will suffer from the mental oppression until that silence explodes into an atomic bomb one day.

The people you surround yourself with may have a huge impact on how you verbally express yourself. If you are constantly surrounded by thugs, you will have the thuggish-street tone. Manipulative people tend to have a toxic and destructive tone. Abusers tend to have a very passive-aggressive and oppressive tone. Traumatised people tend to be in-between hostile, defensive and have a pensive tone. The "almost perfect" people (because no one is perfect) tend to have positive, inspirational, encouraging and very warm tones. All these various tones may form part of your tongue-dentity crisis.

Can you resonate with any of the aforementioned? They say hurt people hurt other people, and broken people will end up breaking other people too. Have you been hurt or broken by something that someone said to you a while ago? Do you remember how strong or sharp that person's tongue was when they insulted or offended you? Do you suffer from post-verbal abuse trauma? Do you recognise the impact that tongue-dentity has on you?

One major narrative that may affect your outcome in life is how you project your expectations. My business mentor once said, "Expectations kill, but projected expectations are even more dangerous. Therefore, you have to be sure to watch exactly what you say." You cannot expect to get that which you cannot give nor attain yourself. You cannot expect a handsome harvest unless you sow some handsome seed, and nurture it until it is ripe and ready. You cannot expect to win the lottery miraculously unless you are actually in it to win it, conversely, being in it doesn't guarantee that you will win it.

You have probably been through numerous relationships that have failed due to one thing or another. You may think that there's something wrong with the people that you date or attract. You may also blame all the failed relationships on all your ex-partners for reasons only you know about. Let's dig a little dipper. Have you ever wondered why your relationships don't work out the way you expect them to? Is it that you are cursed or could it just be sheer misfortune? Yes, I targeted relationships because this is something you and I can both relate to easily. Could your tongue be the route of all the failed encounters? Could your tongue be blocking most of, if not all your blessings? Could it be that you obliviously project words like:

I expect him/her to be financially stable and if not, I'd rather be single.

He/she has to have acquired certain educational qualifications and if not, I'd rather be single.

He/she has to have certain skin tone, height and must have a certain body shape and if not, I'd rather be single.

He/she must have a house, car and a good job and if not, I'd rather be single.

He/she must have minimal or no body count, hold a PhD in perfection, no flaws, no skeletons in the closet, no past, present or future drama, no blemishes, no room for making mistakes and if not, I'd rather be single.

All this might sound funny until you realise that you have been speaking "being single" into existence for so many years. This could be why you have unsuccessful, seasonal or short term relationships. You might justify them by labelling them as "flings" or thinking that it was never meant to be, but the truth of the matter is that you have been blocking all the good fortune.

Moreover, you have no one but yourself to blame for it. Take a moment to think about your "ideal" partner. List down all the ideal qualities and characteristics that you look for in a man or woman versus the reality of meeting and ticking over 50 percent of your checklist. Can you genuinely admit that it is quite challenging to meet someone that matches all your expectations? How often do you take time out to reflect on things that you say on a daily basis, words that you consciously decree and declare? Are you part of the crew that is guilty of voiding their own declarations soon after you make them because you lack faith?

To have faith is to be confident or be very sure of the things you hope for, to be certain of the things you cannot see. So how do you rectify a tongue-dentity crisis with faith? How do you undo or unsay all the negative and unfruitful connotations? How do you avoid proclaiming the wrong things all the time? How do you discipline your tongue? How deep have you dug the tongue-dentity crisis grave? I know I have asked you a lot of intentional questions so far, but the million dollar question is, can it be done? Can the tongue-dentity crisis be dealt with?

The answer has to come from you and you alone. It is your tongue that created or keeps creating the mess/drama, and therefore only you have absolute control over it. You may want to blame it over your upbringing, your circle of friends, your hurt and trauma, but if you do not take the first step to work on it, then who else will? How long can you hold on to the blame policy? How long can you carry the heavy burden? How long can you be the victim?

Well, admitting that there is work to be done or some cleaning up to do is one way of getting started. How long it will take to watch what you say over your life will depend on how it affects your life, and how bad you need change in your life. You can't expect a miracle unless you put some effort and work in it. This is where faith comes in. Faith without works is dead. You may stumble a few times as you try to find your feet. However, everything has a starting point, first you have to crawl, then take baby steps till you find the right balance, then you attempt to walk, and before you know it you will be sprinting even faster than Usain Bolt. Keep the faith.

It took me a while to get it almost right. I am not perfect hence I said almost right. Some days are good and some days are a bit more challenging. There is always something or someone that will trigger how you react and what you then say after being triggered. Those that have been in the same car with me whilst driving will say that I have road rage. However, I like to think that I am quite passionate about safe driving and I expect every road user to at least use some common sense. This is an expectation and, remember, I mentioned earlier on that expectations kill?

This expectation has not been met to date since the day I attained my license. You will come across good road users, and you will also come across extremely bad and dangerous drivers. The latter road users caused me to utter a few ungodly words a few times. Yes I have cursed them a couple of times, but it did not change how badly they drove. In fact, it created unnecessary anger and bad energy in me. Sometimes it would even affect my entire day.

I then realised that I was intentionally releasing bad energy towards the drivers I considered to be dangerous road users. I can only imagine the sort of impact the negative words that I released had on their lives. Sometimes I even wished them dead or to get into a serious accident. Even though this sounds really bad, I kept on doing it out of anger or frustration. Eventually, after a few spiritual convictions, I had to sit down and think about the times when I drove as bad as those dangerous road users did.

At some point I was once a learner, then an anxious new driver. Therefore, making similar mistakes was inevitable.

So I started to question what negative words they projected against me in retaliation. Could it be the reason that I have had a few near car accident misses? What if I did not cover myself with a prayer of protection on a daily basis, would I still be alive today? These are some of the things that you may not think about because they seem trivial until something bad happens.

 Do you want to be another subject that waits until something bad happens prior to fixing it? How many lessons do you want to go through before you actually learn from them?

I continued to reflect on my tongue-dentity crisis regularly, and I eventually found myself correcting my words a lot more. I soon realised that it's ok to say the right things even if you don't feel like it.

It's ok to say positive affirmations even when the circumstances seem impossible.

It's ok to wish your enemy well.

It's ok to encourage others even at your lowest point.

It's ok to say good things about others even if they have nothing good to say about you.

It's ok to defend someone in their absence and avoid being caught up in toxic gossip.

It's ok to say nothing at all especially when you have nothing good or positive to say.

It's ok to forgive those that hurt you and pray for them even though they do the exact opposite.

It's ok to walk away from toxic situations before you get entangled in them.

It's ok to be the odd one out, even if it means being that one in a million who stands for what is right.

It's ok to say no to a tongue-dentity crisis.

It's ok to say enough is enough.

It's ok to recondition your tongue-set and it's never too late to start afresh.

Remember, how you say it is how it will be. Have a reconditioned tongue-set.

Chapter 7

The Family-dentity Crisis

"Family is the best thing you could ever wish for. They are there for you during the ups and the downs. They love and support you no matter what" **– Unknown**

At this point you are either thinking that this is definitely way too farfetched or you are solely agreeing because you have a somewhat perfect family.

Ok, let's try a different perspective.

They say family isn't always blood. It's the people in your life who want you in theirs, the ones who accept you for who you are. The ones who would do anything to see you smile and who love you no matter what. ~ Unknown

This definitely sounds more like how most of us feel about the families we have and the families we choose. They are like branches on a tree, we all grow in different directions yet our roots remain the same.

Family politics feels like a newly exposed Covid-19 global pandemic with no vaccination in the infantry stages to minimise its prevalence. It is a commonality in every household and it is what it is. You have the inevitable family feuds that normally creep up at family gatherings like weddings, birthday celebrations, funerals, baby showers/welcome, baptisms, baby dedications and some pointless meetings that claim to want to unite the family, however, everything ends in turmoil. Amongst your family you will have clusters which are made up of different classes: the upper class, the middle class and the lower class. I belong to one of these, and if you ask me, I do not even understand how these are fairly classified. All I know is you also belong to one of these classes, even though you may not have a full background of how they came about.

When it comes to family matters, we all have an exclusive story to tell. Some come from a perfect family where both mum and dad were present. Everything about their up-bringing is almost a perfect fairy-tale every child wishes for. They were brought up with silver spoons in their mouths. They had the perfect education, the perfect guidance on life, and some even end up with the perfect inheritance.

 On the contrary, even though both parents were present, the family was, the family is and the family will always be a dysfunctional family. No matter how hard the family tries to solve its dysfunctionality, it seems to end up worse than it started.

Some were raised by single parents; either mom or dad alone. Depending on the persona of the parent, the up-bringing was either good, bad or comprises of both good and bad values.

Some had no parents at all, they were raised by other family members due to whatever unfortunate circumstances. They were raised as orphans because their parents were both irresponsible and reckless, or maybe the parents were in tragic accidents.

Some just had it rough and tough and all they know is tough love. Some families are so toxic you'd think they are defunct because you never see them together.

As I have countlessly mentioned, no one on this earth is perfect. Therefore, do not expect your family to behave in a normal or perfect manner. You may be related to your family through blood, but that does not mean that you will all get along very well. I have come across a lot of divided families, some of which have not spoken to each other in ages because of generational rivalry due to lies, gossip and deception. Unfortunately, some millennials are born into this feud and they involuntarily inherit the family drama. You see innocent children not getting along just because their elders misunderstood each other years ago, and therefore they permanently cut blood ties with the rest of the family.

This is an unfortunate deep family-dentity crisis. One that may either build or destroy the forthcoming generations. Denying to afford someone the freedom to experience family accord and love just because of unresolved tensional history is rather selfish and uncalled for. Some of these children grow up missing out on real family values. The family connection is completely lost, and henceforth some people struggle to adapt in the community when they are older, and they may end up being hostile and resistant victims.

I believe that no one is born with hate or rage. These characteristics are taught through watching, listening and absorbing what our parents or guardians do, or what they instruct us to say or do. They normally say an apple does not fall to far from the tree. This means that if the tree is a bad one, you will inherit all the possible bad things. For example, it could be all the toxic habits of an alcoholic, a cheat, a liar, an abuser, a manipulator, a narcissist, and all the other bad attributes you can think of. Nonetheless, if it's a good tree, you will inherit and exhibit all the good traits of that tree.

How factual is this proverb? Do you really think you behave like your parents or ancestors? Are they to blame for your good or bad behaviour? Do you think your dad or your mum's blunders should always justify your family-dentity-crisis? Do you think you hide behind your dysfunctional family in order to mask your own flaws? Should you always take orders or should you stand on your own two feet as a grown human being? Should you start taking responsibility and accountability of your own family-dentity crisis? Is it time to let bygones be bygones and move forward?

You may find yourself in very compromising positions because of the choices you made or keep making. Do you find yourself sacrificing for others yet it is never reciprocated? Are you always taking the bullet for everyone? Are you the go to person when hell breaks loose, but no one is ever around when you need the help?

Are you the bank of everything where everyone keeps withdrawing, but no one ever deposits? Is your glass half full of half empty?

Favouritism is another factor than can cause some serious family-dentity crisis. Every parent has a favourite child and each child has a favourite parent. There's a Joseph in each family clothed with the coat of many colours, whilst everyone else has a regular coat with one colour or two if lucky enough. Every uncle and aunt has a favourite nephew or niece and vice versa. Every grandparent has a favourite grandchild. Favouritism is an inevitable deadly nuisance and you can't avoid it no matter how hard you try. You can argue all you like, but that is the sad truth especially if you are from a very big family. I can bet that you already know who the favourite one in your family is. If you do not know, I suppose that automatically makes you the favourite. However, if you know who the favourite one is, you probably do not care at all, or you are heavily affected by it that you have a bitter sweet relationship with the favourite one.

The sad truth is parents will deny favouritism, but you and I both know that it is very real and it exists. I have seen families fight each other over how much attention and financial support a favourite child is given. Some siblings do not have a close relationship because of accumulated and on-going resentment caused by parents over the favourite child. Some have even gone to the extent of disowning each other, passing death threats and even using black magic (juju) to bewitch the favourite one.

Are you a victim of favouritism in your family? Has this affected your mental health in a negative way? Do you feel unloved, unwanted and unworthy? Are you always the last one to find out important family news? Do you get missed, dismissed or excluded when it's time to make important family decisions? Are you the odd one out? How have you managed to live under the favourite's one shadow for this long? I know I am asking a lot of questions here, but I am hoping that they are provocative enough to make you come out of the closet and face the man in the family-dentity mirror.

Death can cause also some serious family-dentity crisis. It can unite or dismantle a family as the family starts to fight over inheritance of the deceased. It can allow lingering issues to be reconciled as it's a time when everyone is vulnerable, or it can trigger negative dormant issues as emotions will be flying all over the place. Death can bring emotional healing or pain. Death can bring peace or terrorise you depending on the relationship you had with the deceased. It can open a can of worms or be the end to all your troubles and sorrows. It can be the beginning of a new chapter or the end of the road for you. Depending on the nature of your family, death inevitably brings about some form of family-dentity crisis.

Hurt people hurt people. Hurt family members will hurt other family members. Some will even go to the extent of creating physical barriers, emotional and mental barriers. If you are hurting from past or recent trauma and you haven't healed completely, you might be subconsciously hurting other people. You might be taking out your anger or frustration on the wrong people. You might also be blocking the very people that actually have your best interest at heart.

Many a times, you might let pride and arrogance get the best of you and therefore you do not allow others to positively criticise you. You take every critic as an attack. You do not see the log in your own eye yet you see the specs in others. You don't think you do any wrong, but others do. You want to preach to the congregation, counsel and give advice to the broken and hurt nation yet you do not take any advice from anyone. You think you know it all, you have it all figured out, your opinions should and must always be heard and actioned all the time.

You are never apologetic even when you're at fault. You always try and brush things under the carpet instead of dealing with the issues at hand. Whenever things go wrong, you distance yourself from the rest of the family until you think it's ok to spontaneously reappear without any equitable explanation. FYI, this is what we class as extreme "toxic" family-dentity behaviour. Sometimes you try and befriend those you're not fighting with, and you gossip with them about the ones you are fighting with to make yourself look like a Good Samaritan. You even start to reveal information you were told in confidence by others, just to try and buy love from them. Are you a Good Samaritan or a Gossip Samaritan?

At times you use manipulative language to get your way all the time. You twist your words and their words so that you are always right and they are at fault. You are always the victim. No one understands you. No one cares for you. No one checks up on you. You feel like you don't belong to that family. Sometimes you think you were adopted. It's either your way or it's the high way.

Does this sound like you or someone in your family? Can you resonate with this family-dentity crisis? Is it too close to home?

How do you accept or help them realise and accept this crisis? Is it one of those non-starter situations? Are you experiencing a bowl of mixed emotions right now? Are you in denial? Are you willing to work on those damaged family-ships or are you going to bury it and just swiftly move on as always?

Do you think it's beyond repair? Is it too late to apologise even if your apology might not be accepted?

Why are things the way they are in your family? Why is there so much drama and chaos? How come people can't just get along, love one another, help each other, inspire, encourage, motivate and just be one big happy family?

Why does jealousy and greed control your family? Why is there so much animosity amongst the family? Why do you compete against each other? Why does the spirit of disunity hold everyone down? Why does money separate your family?

Remember I mentioned that each family has its own family-dentity crisis? Even the British Royals have some serious family-dentity crisis. So what then? How do we solve this crisis? The question is, can you and are you willing to solve it within your own family?

I have my own family-dentity crisis just like you and everyone else. There are some family members that I do not speak and haven't spoken to for personal reasons. However, that does not mean that they aren't family, nor do I hate them. I just do not agree with certain behaviour and the family politics at hand. They might have different perspectives, but I still highly regard them as my family. We are like branches on a tree, we all grow in different directions yet our roots remain the same.

Listen, I could go on about family matters because it is a very broad and sensitive topic. There a lot of things that I didn't address intentionally because they may cause world war five. A war even bigger than the current Covid-19 pandemic and I still want to live and enjoy life. You know this is true because it is in your family too.

Nonetheless, no matter the issues within my family-dentity crisis, I choose "peace" and I will always choose peace. They say "anything that costs you your peace is too expensive" and trust me, this is very true. I found that peace can take you a very long way. Peace can let you forgive easily and let go the unnecessary strongholds without taking much from you. Peace can let you accept your flaws and of those around you. Peace can allow you to discern the good and the bad, and you still choose to see the good in all the bad. Peace can motivate you to be a Good Samaritan because there's more joy in giving than in receiving.

Peace can allow you to love the family that dislikes you and still manage to extend a right hand, even though it is not reciprocated. Peace can allow you to be brave enough to protect your mental health without blaming it on the toxic ones. Peace will allow you to understand that there's a season and a reason for everything. Therefore, no matter the family-dentity crisis, you'll not be broken forever.

You'll find strength to love, strength to be joyful, strength to fight against the fiery darts against you, and strength to accept the things you can and cannot change.

"I am leaving you with a gift – peace of mind and heart. And the peace I give is a gift the world cannot give. So don't be troubled or afraid." John 14:27 (NLT)

It is your family-dentity crisis, your identity crisis, so what are you going to do about it?

Chapter 8

The Butterfly-dentity Analogy

A butterfly is one of the most beautiful creatures in the world, but it doesn't become a fully grown butterfly overnight. It has to go through a full life cycle, just like you and I have to go through a developmental process from conception till we eventually die.

The life cycle of a butterfly goes through a process called metamorphosis. This is where the butterfly goes through four development stages; from an egg to a larva, then to a pupa, and finally, it turns into an adult butterfly. Stage one is when it is just an egg. At this point, it is just a plain egg, with no identity and no form. There is a fifty-fifty probability of life or death at this stage. The egg stage is where you find most people, and some struggle to move on from here. They maybe be naïve to the fact that they are stagnant, they have no identity or they may be bursting with excuses to make themselves feel better. If you are at this stage in your adult life, you are definitely facing an identity crisis. So, are you going to develop onto stage two or not?

Stage two is when the egg develops and hatches into a larvae or caterpillar. If you were to come across the larvae at this stage, you would struggle to identify that is it a butterfly in progress. Though it has progressed onto the next stage, it is still far from being correctly identified. Depending on the nature and circumstances of development, it may survive this stage or fail to develop any further. Are you currently at the larvae or caterpillar stage? How long were you at the egg stage and what challenges did you come across? Did you manage to identify and separate the grass from the weeds? What does the larvae stage of your identity crisis currently look like?

At stage three, the caterpillar feeds on its eggshell from where it hatches from in order to grow and develop further. It then goes on to feed on leaves which are full of all necessary nutrients required for its growth. It also sheds off its old skin several times as part of the growth process. The caterpillar feeds until it grows big enough to move onto the next stage. At this stage you may come across a lot of issues and challenges as you constantly search deep within. You may open a can of worms which you have to assertively take control of. You may need to drop dead wood, keep and pick up relevant wood.

At stage four, It goes through a process called chrysalis were it forms a protective layer around itself and it develops into pupa. It undergoes a series of changes and after roughly fifteen days, it emerges from the chrysalis stage into a beautiful adult butterfly. At this stage, it pumps fluid into its wings to make them stronger and to expand. After a while, the wings become stronger and the butterfly is able to fly.

As a butterfly goes through metamorphosis, you also go through a series of changes in your life that either shape or break you depending on how desperate you are at each stage to identifying and unlocking your hidden treasure. You go through childhood, adolescence, adulthood and then you eventually die. What you do in-between life and death, defines your real character.

You must realise that you have to go through some deep pruning as you embark on the "finding yourself journey." Sometimes you have to endure the most painful and inexcusable experiences to help define you. Sometimes you are privileged enough to be born with a silver spoon in your mouth. This means you do not endure the harsh conditions that someone else goes through. Nonetheless, everything comes to an end. It ends differently for you and I. You reap what you sow.

Every road leads to a particular destination. It may be a good destination or a complete dead end. Do you stop moving when you come across a dead end? Do you follow any diversion signs in place and possibly use your "satnav" to reroute until you get to your intended destination? My spiritual mentor (Min G) once shared a word of encouragement called, "It is but a light thing." As hard as this may be to digress and digest, sometimes what we complicate in life is but a light thing. The light thing could easily be turning off the bad and switching on the good. The light thing could be getting rid of the toxic and allowing the harmless to dominate. The light thing could be nurturing on the positive and shying away from the negative vibes.

Furthermore, my life coach and business mentor Itayi Garande, a bespoke No 1 Amazon best seller always reminds me that it is all about reconditioning of the mind – "eyesight versus mind-sight." In one of his books, he highlights how he lived with bitterness about past relationships, broken friendships, failed attempts, shattered hopes and dreams.

"Shingie, the reason most people never achieve their full potential is simply because they give up when faced with tragedy, pain and suffering... Life was never meant to be easy. It is a constant struggle, fighting tragedy and enjoying happy moments." This mind-blowing extract from "Reconditioning: Change your life in one minute" made me realise that the tragedy he was talking about is an identity crisis.

Chapter 9

Finding Your Sweet Spot In An Identity Crisis

F inding your sweet spot in this identity crisis journey will have nipping moments of realisation. You will find yourself crying, laughing, cursing (please repent immediately after this) laughing or rejoicing. You may kiss your teeth too as you relive some memories you thought you had long buried. However, you have to be desperate enough to unlock self-awareness in order to "fix" or begin the "work" on yourself. No one has to force you to do it. It has to come deeply from within. That's where the magic and the matrix is.

Have you ever been so desperate for oxygen you felt like if you had one more second without it you possibly wouldn't be here today reading this book? Lack or depletion of oxygen has different complications ranging from irreversible brain damage to fatality. If you are not desperate to unlock the treasure within you; you might be amongst individuals that we refer to as "the walking dead." They are alive, but in reality they are dead. They are motionless. They have no goals, no ambitions, and no prospects.

You may have "pressure" to do certain things by a certain age. Yes, you know exactly what I am implying. A lot of women unfortunately fall under pressure to get married by a certain age. Once you reach your "thirties," you're told that the biological clock starts ticking. "Girl your options are now limited, beauty fades and no man fancies an old chick. Just have your baby now and you'll be fine. Time is running out. No one will find you attractive after thirty-five." The list of these negative statements is endless, and inevitably you are peer pressured to settle for less.

Unfortunately, I have seen a lot of women fall under the settling bracket. The so called "advisors" or "they- the elders" make it seem like it is the end of the world. If you miss this certain window period, your world is over. "My people perish for lack of knowledge," Hosea 4:6. This congruently resonates to ignorance or illiteracy re self-awareness.

Man fall under a lot of pressure too. It mostly has to do with being able to provide financially. It seems as though they are exempt when it comes to getting married or starting a family before they reach their thirties. The financial pressure may deter them from pursuing serious and committed relationships. Moreover, they feel that they have to have a certain amount of savings in the bank prior to settling down. This has led to a lot of toxic relationships, break-ups, high divorce rates, and hit and runs.

If you are not careful about the voice(s) you subscribe to, you will be caught in an identity crisis where everyone dictates your life, the pace and how it should be.

Chapter 10

Unlock The Hidden Treasure Within You

"The graveyard is the richest place on earth, because it is here that you will find all the hopes and dreams that were never fulfilled, the books that were never written, the songs that were never sung, the inventions that were never shared, the cures that were never discovered, all because someone was too afraid to take that first step, keep with the problem, or determined to carry out their dream" **– Les Brown**

S o far you should have an idea of what your identity crisis is or could be, and if not, could you be in denial that you have one?

You have probably uncovered some identity crisis that I have not addressed in this book. Make a list of them and decide how you are going to progressively work on them. Some things are easier said than done, however, you do not want to live with regrets for the rest of your life. It is never too late to start. It's never too late to work on your identity crisis as soon as you acknowledge it. It's never too late to detach and distance accordingly. It's never too late move on and keep moving.

Unlocking your potential requires a lot determination, responsibility and accountability. There is a lot that is in you that is waiting to be extracted and put to use. You cannot continue to let fear or any limiting beliefs bind you and steal your great destiny away from you. You have to face the man in the mirror and start peeling the onion layers off one by one until you get to the bottom of it all.

I heavily rely on one of my favourite scriptures; Ecclesiastes 3 vs 1-8. It really touches on every aspect of life. They say one man's meat is another man's poison.

This is definitely my meat:

1. **There is a time for everything, and a reason for every activity under the heavens**

It may have taken you this long to identify, acknowledge or deal with your identity crisis. Each day has a lesson, each lesson has a reason, each reason has a season, and each season has a destiny. Do not be too hard on yourself because there is a time and reason behind it all. Each season will be accompanied by trials and tribulations as you embark on this journey. However, what matters the most is the next step you are willing to take in order to unlock the treasure within you – self-awareness, self-care, self-love and your true identity. Each destiny has YOU written all over it. Just do it.

2. **A time to be born and a time to die; a time to plant and a time to pluck up that which is planted**

Appreciate the gift of life whilst you still can. If you are pregnant with ideas, make sure you take all the necessary strategies prior to birthing them. Start and always finish your projects. Do not stop halfway and move on to the next chapter before completion.

Inevitably you are going to die. Make sure you have lived and embraced life before that time comes. Every living thing has an expiry date. Even plants wither and eventually die.

Plant good seed and yield good results. When you make good investments, you will eventually have handsome returns. As we do with crop rotation, be ready to uproot the seasonal plants and prepare for the next season.

3. A time kill, and a time to heal; a time to break down and a time to build up

Kill (not literally) every negative and bad spirit. Kill the unnecessary relationships and anything deterring your progression. Heal completely before you move on. Heal from the pain, the trauma, the rejection, the abuse, the deception, the breakup, and the toxic wounds caused by others and including you.

Renovations require some tearing down. There are things about you, your environment and your circles that will need several changes. You will tear down some good ideas and connections in order to build the best ones. More importantly, you will tear the old man (body, mind, spirit and soul) to build a new man – you. This will be a reconditioned you for the better. Build wisely, build stronger and build fearlessly.

4. **A time to weep, and a time to laugh; a time to mourn and a time to dance**

Save the last dance as all good things come to those who wait patiently. Tears of sorrow as you discover some unsettling truths about your identity crisis will be shed. Cry it all out because accumulation of sorrow creates room for explosive disaster. It is very normal and healthy too to mourn. Let that river of tears flow now before it drowns you emotionally.

5. **A time to cast away stones, and a time to gather them; a time to embrace and a time to refrain from embracing**

You may be all over the place as you discover things about you. You may decide to seek professional help or deal with it personally as you see fit. You may reopen some long closed dockets as you try to get a clearer vision of past events. They say never put all eggs in one basket because it may be all over before it even begins. So until you are very comfortable in your own skin, it is ideal to try different avenues to identify your basic needs. You can do this until you find a compatible lock and key; an agonistic set of keys. You may also need to let go of certain things for now until it's time to put them together again.

Embrace the need to work on you. Embrace the importance of self-discovery. Embrace the long hours you may have to put into that project. Embrace the patience you will need for that relationship to work. Embrace the reconciliation and restoration process. Embrace that life maybe unfair at times. Embrace that you are unique.

Nonetheless, refrain from the pressure that may come with embracing, instead manage it wisely so that you don't fall into another identity crisis. Remove the cob webs step by step, and take time off to reboot if need be. Refrain from overdoing, overthinking and refrain from being a wonder woman or wonder man. Refrain from the burn-out that comes with the "hustle."

6. A time to get, and a time to lose; a time to keep and a time to cast away

You may need to search deeper into certain aspects of your identity crisis. You will come across a lot of good and bad things. You have to filter out the bad clutter and keep the necessary stuff only. You may need to give up on stagnant and unfruitful habits. Give up on dead wood. Give up on procrastination and laziness. Give up on the pretentious life you have been living. You cannot have the cake and eat it to. Somethings just have to go and this depends on you.

7. A time to rend, and a time to sew; a time to keep silence and a time to speak

Not everything requires your two cents. Sometimes it pays more to be silent. Sometimes you say more when you say nothing at all. Know exactly when to speak because life and death lie in the power of the tongue. Tame your tongue and know when to swallow your words and when to share them. Speak life, speak positivity and always speak the truth for the truth shall set you free.

8. A time to love and a time to hate; a time for war and a time for peace

Love surpasses hate. Love the way you want to be loved. Love no matter how impossible or difficult it is because we are commanded to love one another as we love ourselves. If you do not agree, please take it up with your creator. Hate or be angry, but do not let the sun go down on your anger. Fight for your destiny, fight for your purpose, fight for your life, fight for your identity and be at peace with all the decisions you make because they will identify you.

Chapter 11

The Man In The Mirror.

Sometimes you have *you* to blame for some of the things that have happened to you, that are currently happening to you, or that will happen to you. In as much as we can try to shift the blame onto others, the question is, how much of the damage, or identity crisis is down to you?

You engaged into some of the situation-ships fully seeing the red flags, but you blatantly ignored them and switched on the blind switch. Apparently love is blind.

You knew it was going to end in tears, but you thought you could manage or change the situation, and now you are sitting there nursing your heart for the umpteenth time.

You knew it was a bad idea, but you still went ahead with it and the inevitable happened.

You knew it wasn't the right time to go ahead with the plan, project or the proposition, but you gave into peer pressure.

You knew it was a dead end, but you convinced yourself that there was a light at the end of the tunnel.

You knew right from wrong, but you fully decided on your own downfall.

You knew it wasn't from God, but you decided to rewrite Jeremiah 29:11 which states "For I know the plans I have for you," declares the Lord, "plans to prosper you and not to harm you, plans to give you hope and a future."

You knew he/she was a wolf dressed in sheep's skin, but you gave him/her the benefit of the doubt.

You knew that you did not know enough to make an informed decision, but you convinced yourself that you will cross the bridge when you get there, only to find out that there wasn't any bridge to cross in the first place.

You knew it was a can full of worms, but you thought the worms were harmless and you opened it anyway.

You knew you were pushing forbidden boundaries and limits, but you cared not.

You knew it was time to let go, but you convinced yourself that you invested a lot of time and energy into the job, the friendship, the relationship, the entanglement and any other "ship" you can think of, and therefore you held on to it.

Even after you found out, and everything was out in the open, you caught them red handed, the evidence was in black and white, the jurisdiction had pleaded the outcome, you still decided on your own fate.

It is your identity crisis after all. What now?

Learn to accept your flaws, and accept your mistakes.

Accept your blemishes, and accept your foolishness.

Accept your ignorance, and accept your vulnerability.

Accept your weaknesses, and accept your blindness.

Acceptance is a good place to deal with the man in the mirror – *you*.

Chapter 12

Post Identity Crisis Questions

"Character is like pregnancy. It cannot be hidden forever"
–African proverb

Well done for going through the entire book and getting to this stage. It is now time to attempt those questions again, and to evaluate your progress. Be as honest as you can.

1. Who am I?
2. What is my identity?
3. What do I want out of life?
4. Where do I see myself physically, mentally, and spiritually in the next few hours, days, weeks, months and years to come?
5. What is my current status: health, finance, career, relationships, friends and family?
6. What do I believe in?
7. What do I want and what do I need?
8. What are my expectations?
9. What makes me happy and what makes me sad?
10. What are my weaknesses and what are my strengths?
11. How far am I willing to go to change my life?

12. Who am I?

Note: You can answer these questions as many times as you want. Remember it is a progressive journey.